John Locke's
Political Philosophy

John Locke's Political Philosophy

Eight Studies by J. W. Gough

Emeritus Fellow of Oriel College, Oxford

SECOND EDITION

OXFORD
AT THE CLARENDON PRESS
1973

Oxford University Press, Ely House, London W. 1

GLASGOW   NEW YORK   TORONTO   MELBOURNE   WELLINGTON
CAPE TOWN   IBADAN   NAIROBI   DAR ES SALAAM   LUSAKA   ADDIS ABABA
DELHI   BOMBAY   CALCUTTA   MADRAS   KARACHI   LAHORE   DACCA
KUALA LUMPUR   SINGAPORE   HONG KONG   TOKYO

First Edition 1950
Second Edition 1973

Printed in Great Britain
at the University Press, Oxford
by Vivian Ridler
Printer to the University

PREFACE TO THE SECOND EDITION

SINCE I first began work on this book, Locke and his writings, published and unpublished, have been the subject of a remarkable outpouring of books and articles, as may be gathered from the bibliography, 'Forty Years of Work on John Locke (1929–1969)', which appeared in the *Philosophical Quarterly*, xx (1970), pp. 258–68, and has since been supplemented by the launching of the *Locke Newsletter*. Only a small part of this outpouring has been concerned with Locke's political thought, but it has included a diversity of novelties. A principal cause of this intense interest in Locke has been the greater accessibility of the Lovelace collection of his manuscripts since they were acquired by the Bodleian Library. Apart from the work (done some years previously, when the manuscripts were still in private ownership) of B. Rand, and of R. I. Aaron and J. Gibb, on the early drafts of the *Essay on Human Understanding*, I believe that two of the studies in this book (on the Law of Nature and on Toleration) were the first publications to be based on an examination, albeit rather cursory, of some parts of this wealth of new material. Since then scholars from all over the world—from India and Japan, from America, from France, Germany, and Italy, not to speak of Great Britain itself—have been, and still are, hard at work on it. There has been a new biography of Locke, and critical editions have appeared of a number of his unpublished works; apart from his correspondence, on which Dr. E. S. de Beer has been engaged for some years, I believe that practically all Locke's writings of any importance are now in print.

Not all the new work on Locke has been the outcome of

this new material. Some has resulted from the fresh application of critical technique, or from new-fashioned methods
of analysis, to the established corpus of his writings. Some
of this work has thrown fresh light on Locke, or corrected
long-standing mistakes about him. Some of it, on the other
hand, has been paradoxical, not to say rather absurd.
The effect of it all on myself has been to persuade me to
modify in various ways some of the views I expressed in
the first edition of this book, but not to abandon my belief
that the primary historical significance of Locke's political
thought is his support of constitutional government and
opposition to absolute monarchy. He showed what he himself valued by writing 'Pax ac Libertas' on the title-page
of the French translation of his *Civil Government* (see J.
Harrison and P. Laslett, *The Library of John Locke* (Oxford,
1965), Plate 6). By constitutional government of course is
meant constitutional government as understood in the
seventeenth century, and certainly it is misleading either to
read back into Locke modern liberal-democratic assumptions, or to criticize him for lacking them. What I must
confess I am not entirely happy about is the title of this
book. Whether or not Locke developed what can be called
a political philosophy, and whether or not his intention
in writing, and subsequently publishing, *Two Treatises of
Government* was to give expression to it, are debatable
points. Was he not rather making a controversial contribution to the practical politics of his day? These questions apart, it has been objected that the title is not an
accurate label for the contents of the book. But to change
the title might suggest that this is a new book, whereas in
fact it is an old book revised. Substantial parts of it have
been rewritten, or rearranged, but much if it remains the
same. In the first edition there was an Appendix containing
Addenda and *Corrigenda* to Fox Bourne's version of Locke's

Essay concerning Toleration of 1667. This Appendix is now omitted. Some of its more noteworthy points have been incorporated in my eighth study, and the text of Locke's *Essay* itself, with comments on the four different versions of it, is available in C. A. Viano's edition of Locke's *Scritti Editi e Inediti sulla Tolleranza* (Turin, 1961), which is at any rate not less accessible to readers than Fox Bourne's *Life of Locke*, published in 1876 and long out of print.

J. W. G.

Oriel College, Oxford
July 1972

PREFACE TO THE FIRST EDITION

THESE studies do not pretend to form a continuous or exhaustive account of the whole of Locke's political philosophy. They are concerned with certain parts of it which seemed worth discussing afresh. They are connected, however, because the topics they cover are contiguous, and sometimes overlap. An obvious drawback to discussing such topics in separate studies is that, unless the writer interrupts the argument by leaving gaps, he can hardly avoid repeating himself. Of these alternatives I think repetition is the less tiresome, because each study can then be self-contained; but I have in fact tried to compromise, by giving each topic only one main discussion, and treating it elsewhere more summarily, with references in the notes to the study where the main discussion occurs.

Apart from some general reflections, I have confined myself mainly to the place occupied by these topics in Locke's own thought. My first study, on the Law of Nature, does indeed begin with a couple of paragraphs on the previous history of this law, because it seemed that some such opening could hardly be avoided; but I have reduced this to the very briefest sketch, because excellent short outlines of its history are to be found elsewhere, and to write anything like a full account of the Law of Nature would be an immense task entirely outside the range of this book. Nor have I attempted to trace the sources from which Locke may have derived his ideas, on this or other subjects, partly because that too would demand a book to itself, and partly because it has already been done by Mr. A. H. Maclean, of Peterhouse, Cambridge, in a dissertation which I had the honour of examining for the degree of Ph.D. in that university, and of which a section (on George Lawson) has already been published in the *Cambridge Historical Journal* for 1947. Numerous critics of Locke have agreed in saying that Locke's political ideas were not original, but Mr. Maclean has been the first, as far as I know, to discuss their origins in detail, and I should like to take this opportunity of acknowledging my indebtedness for much that I learned by reading his work.

One of the chief points of interest in Locke's treatment of the Law of Nature is the question of its cognition, to which his answer was that we know it by the light of nature. This, of course, is a familiar phrase, common enough to be given a paragraph and a definition to itself in the *Oxford English Dictionary*, and already established in the language long before Locke's time. We shall see that Locke offers an explanation of what he means by this phrase in one of his hitherto unpublished set of Latin essays on the Law of Nature among the Lovelace Papers now in the Bodleian Library.

Another question which already had a lengthy history before Locke came to deal with it, and on which a massive body of literature is in existence, is that of religious toleration, which forms the subject of my concluding study. This was a question much canvassed in England, particularly among the Puritan sectaries about the time of the Interregnum. From his earliest years Locke must have been familiar with their discussions, and in fact, as we shall see, one of his first extant writings was intended as a contribution to the controversy then being waged on this subject. Here again, apart from an extremely cursory sketch by way of introduction, I confine myself to Locke's own views, without attempting any investigation of their precise affiliations. I may perhaps point out, however, that the word 'indifferent', which recurs so frequently in the works of Locke and others, was already of old standing as a religious term; the *O.E.D.* quotes examples of its use in 1563 and 1576, and 'adiaphoron' was even earlier. I should also add that I have said nothing about the brief essay on toleration composed by Locke during his stay in France, which he wrote in shorthand (together with several essays on other topics) in his Journal for 1676, and which has now been transcribed by Dr. W. von Leyden, of the University of Durham.

My seventh study (on Political Trusteeship) which ranges more widely than Locke himself, was originally published in 1939 as an article in *Politica*, and I am grateful to the London School of Economics and Political Science for permission to reprint it here in a revised form. I should also like to record my thanks to the Provost of Oriel, Dr. G. N. Clark, who read the whole book in typescript and gave me several valuable hints, and to my father-in-law, the Revd. Dr. P. J. Maclagan, who read my first draft, and drew my attention to a number of places where my arrangement and phraseology needed clarification.

J. W. G.

Oriel College, Oxford
June 1949

CONTENTS

I

THE LAW OF NATURE

THE Law of Nature, which was the foundation-stone of Locke's political philosophy, is one of the oldest concepts in the history of political thought. Its origins can be traced back to the distinctions Aristotle drew between law which is particular and positive, enacted for this or that city, and law which is universal and according to nature; and between natural justice which is universally valid, and justice which is legal, or conventional.[1] The notion of a universal natural justice was developed by the Stoics, who taught that in virtue of the common human faculty of reason all men should be citizens of a cosmopolis under a common law of reason, instead of being divided politically into separate cities. From the Stoics the idea of a law of nature, which was a law of reason, valid for all men because of their common human nature, passed in turn to the Roman lawyers, who transmitted it to the Christian fathers, and to the successive schools of lawyers and scholastic philosophers in the Middle Ages. To the Romans it remained an ideal, and never became a practical law—no Roman jurist asserted the principle upheld later by medieval lawyers and their followers, that positive law could be overridden by natural law—but it influenced their interpretation and application of law, and acquired a status in the body of their jurisprudence. In the Christian era the law of nature was associated with the cognate idea of the law, or will, of God; and reason, which distinguishes man

[1] *Rhetoric*, 1373 b. 4, *Nic. Ethics*, 1134 b. 18.

from the lower animals, was looked on as the faculty given him by God to be his moral guide. The relationship between these ideas was worked out by medieval lawyers, who also studied the whole body of Roman law, including the tradition of natural law it contained. They treated it as a living system which could be adapted and applied to current needs, with the result that they gave rise to the notion of a practical law, Roman in origin, which could be called natural in virtue of its universality and conformity with rational principles.

As natural law was developed in this way it produced in turn the idea that genuine natural law should be something more purely rational than the actual body of law studied and applied by civilians and canonists, so that by the seventeenth and eighteenth centuries there had grown up, especially in Germany, a great school of *Naturrecht*, which engaged in academic study of 'all forms of human society capable of developing a law or of being regulated by law'.[1] The field of this study included the state and its government and organization, and the relationships between states in peace and war. It also included all kinds of groups other than the state, provinces and municipalities, churches and commercial companies, and their relationship to the state and to each other. Two of the greatest writers of this school in the seventeenth century were Grotius and Pufendorf; Locke knew their work and commended it (and especially Pufendorf's) as suitable for a gentleman's education. Besides these great European writers, Locke also knew the work of a number of Englishmen who had expounded the same tradition. Notable

[1] For the history of natural law see A. P. d'Entrèves, *Natural Law* (1951). There is an excellent short summary in E. Barker, Introduction to O. Gierke, *Natural Law and the Theory of Society* (Cambridge, 1934), pp. xxxiv–l, and another in B. F. Wright, *The American Interpretation of Natural Law* (Cambridge, Mass., 1931), pp. 3–12.

among these in an earlier generation was Richard Hooker, whom Locke had studied deeply and often quoted; more recently, Richard Cumberland had published a Latin treatise on the law of nature in reply to Hobbes, and Locke must have known this, for he had a copy of it in his library, and his friend James Tyrrell later published an abridgement of it in English under the title, *A Brief Disquisition of the Law of Nature*. Apart from these and other treatises of the same type, the notion of a law of nature or reason was popularized by the sermons of clergy such as Whichcote, Barrow, and Tillotson, whose preaching Locke admired. He was thoroughly familiar with the whole tradition of which this school of thought was the culmination, so that it formed the inevitable starting-point from which he would naturally approach the subject-matter of moral and political philosophy.

This attitude Locke shared with the great mass of thinkers of his day. Hobbes had shocked his generation by his view that man was under no moral obligation in the state of nature,[1] and had evoked a chorus of protest from all sides in support of the traditional view that the law of nature is real and binding. What was the law of nature supposed to contain? Medieval jurists had regarded it as a genuine law, superior to all positive or man-made law, so that judgements given or legislation passed in contravention of its principles were null. In England, by the second half of the seventeenth century, though the

[1] Professor Howard Warrender, developing a view put forward in 1938 by A. E. Taylor, has contested this interpretation of Hobbes, arguing that Hobbes believed there were genuine obligations in the state of nature. But this view has been widely challenged, and Warrender himself admits that the obligations recognized by Hobbes differed from moral obligations as ordinarily understood. See H. Warrender, *The Political Philosophy of Hobbes* (Oxford, 1957), especially Part I; also articles in K. C. Brown (ed.), *Hobbes Studies* (Oxford, 1965), for some of the subsequent controversy on this question.

principle of the legislative sovereignty of parliament was still only imperfectly grasped, it was no longer possible to maintain (as had been done not so long before) that the courts should refuse to apply legislation which they judged to be contrary to reason or natural law. The law of nature was ceasing to be thought of as a concrete set of judicial or political rules for practical application, and was coming to be regarded rather as a system of ethical principles. It was a guide to all human conduct, including the conduct of rulers and magistrates, whose actions should be tested in its light; but it was 'unwritten, and so nowhere to be found but in the minds of men'.[1]

It was, pre-eminently, 'a law of reason'. Reason was the peculiarly human faculty, possessed by no other creature; it was a faculty, moreover, which man shared with God, and which had been given him by God 'to be the rule betwixt man and man'.[2] The law of nature could thus also be called the law of God, for it was a declaration of the will of God.[3] But these ideas, though related, could also be distinguished, for the law of nature was a law of reason, while the will of God, or law of God, was made known to man by authoritative revelation. This point had also long since given rise to a problem of interpretation. Man must obey God's commands, for what God commands is good and righteous. But does God make something good and righteous simply by commanding it, and is the law of nature, therefore, only God's positive law? This had been the nominalist point of view. Or does God himself, as the realists argued, act from the necessity of reason, so that the content of the law of nature is determined ultimately, not by the fact that God has commanded it, but by its inherent reasonableness? Might it not therefore be

---

[1] *Second Treatise*, § 136; cf. Rom. ii. 14, 15.
[2] *Second Treatise*, § 172.   [3] § 135.

reasonable and binding even if God commanded something else, or if he did not exist at all? If the nominalist view is accepted, God himself seems indistinguishable from an arbitrary despot; but the realist doctrine appears to limit his omnipotence.[1]

I think Locke would have regarded this ancient dispute as an unreal and rather trivial one. Morality, he would have said, indeed consists in obedience to God's commands, and there can be no idea of morality without the idea of God. But morality is not merely obedience to arbitrary commands, nor does God in fact issue arbitrary commands. What he commands is rational and righteous because such is his nature.[2] Behind this dispute, however, there lay a more serious problem, which was really one of epistemology. The law of nature is a law of reason, but how does reason discover it? On the one hand, man might treat Holy Scripture as an inspired revelation of the divine will, and in the seventeenth century hardly anyone would have thought of the Bible in any other way. By itself, however, this might simply mean the uncritical acceptance of dogmatic instruction, leaving little, if any, scope for the faculty of reason. Some authorities, on the other hand, held that the law of nature could be found in the universal agreement of nations, or, if this seemed too sweeping, of 'the most civilized nations'. But who is to judge which nations are civilized, or which are more civilized than others, and, for that matter, why do different peoples or nations agree on certain questions? Many thinkers in the seventeenth century could not rest satisfied with this ultimately relativist view, which treated the moral law as something of

[1] On the controversy between realists and nominalists as to whether natural law was binding because it was reasonable or because it was the command of God see O. Gierke (tr. Maitland), *Political Theories of the Middle Age*, pp. 172–3.

[2] Cf. *Essay concerning Human Understanding*, II. xxi. 49.

purely human manufacture, in which God had had nothing to do. A number of English writers, notably some of the Cambridge Platonists, propounding the theory that God planted certain principles, practical as well as speculative, in men's minds, and that the faculty of reason, with which man was also endowed, enabled him to ascertain the law of nature by consideration of these innate principles. Locke demolished this theory in the opening chapters of his *Essay concerning Human Understanding*, but it is not clear that he had fully thought out a satisfactory alternative. Hooker had said that 'the main principles of Reason are in themselves apparent', and 'in every kind of knowledge some such grounds there are, as that being proposed the mind doth presently embrace them as free from all possibility of error, clear and manifest without proof'.[1] This answer to the problem evidently impressed Locke favourably, for in 1681 he thought it worth noting down in his Journal.

While he rejected innate ideas, Locke at the same time undoubtedly believed, and repeated several times, that moral truths were certain, and as capable of demonstration as mathematics. He first stated this belief in his Journal for 24 June 1681,[2] where he contrasted on the one hand 'physique, polity and prudence', which 'are not capable of demonstration, but a man is principally helped in them by the history of matter of fact, and a sagacity of enquiring

[1] *Eccl. Pol.* i. viii. 5.

[2] Printed in Lord King, *Life of John Locke* (Bohn's ed., 1858), pp. 121–2. This passage, incidentally, makes it clear that in Locke's view the law of nature, though it bulked more largely in the *Second Treatise of Government* than in any other of his published works, essentially belonged to morals rather than to politics. It was, in fact, the moral foundation on which the political superstructure was to be built, the moral criterion by which political action was to be tested. See also Locke's Journal for 26 June 1681, printed in R. I. Aaron and J. Gibb, *Early Draft of Essay* (Oxford, 1936), p. 116.

into probable causes, and finding out an analogy in their operations and effects', and on the other 'the truths of mathematics and morality', which are certain, 'whether men make true mathematical figures, or suit their actions to the rules of morality or no'. Thus, 'it is every man's duty to be just, whether there be any such thing as a just man in the world or no', in the same way as 'the three angles of a triangle are equal to two right ones, . . . whether there be any such figure as a triangle existing in the world or no'. On the other hand, 'whether this course in public or private matters will succeed well,—whether rhubarb will purge or quinquina cure an ague' are matters merely of experience and probability, not of 'certain knowledge or demonstration'.

In the *Essay* Locke explained that the kind of demonstration he thought possible in ethical matters would result from the combination of certain ideas (mixed modes, as he called them).[1] For example, 'where there is no property there is no injustice' is 'a proposition as certain as any demonstration in Euclid: for the idea of property being a right to anything, and the idea to which the name "injustice" is given being the invasion or violation of that right, it is evident that these ideas being thus established, . . . I can as certainly know this proposition to be true, as that a triangle has three angles equal to two right ones'. Another example he gives is 'No government allows absolute liberty'; government involves laws, and absolute liberty means that anyone is free to do what he pleases, and these ideas are obviously incompatible. Locke suggested that 'the idea of a supreme Being, infinite in power, goodness and wisdom, whose workmanship we are, and on whom we depend; and the idea of ourselves, as understanding, rational creatures, being such as are clear in us,

[1] *Essay*, III. xi. 15, 16; IV. iii. 18–20, iv. 7 ff., xii. 8.

would, I suppose, if duly considered and pursued, afford such foundations of our duty and rules of action as might place *morality* amongst the *sciences capable of demonstration*'. The task of constructing such a science of ethics would be difficult, because its ideas are complex and of uncertain signification, but he declared himself confident that these obstacles could be overcome to a great extent by establishing clear definitions and adhering to them 'steadily and constantly'.

Locke did not, however, fulfil the task he here suggested, and the examples he gave amount to no more than defining the meaning of certain terms and then drawing tautologous conclusions from their logical incompatibility. But morality is not, like mathematics, a self-contained world bounded by its own definitions, and it would require a different sort of proof from this to show that justice is a duty, or what actions are just. Locke's friends and readers repeatedly urged him to expound his views on this subject at greater length,[1] and though he never published anything more, a small octavo sheet in the Lovelace Collection of his papers (now in the Bodleian Library), headed *Morality*, of uncertain date but written probably during the last years of his life, apparently represents an attempt to substantiate his thesis.[2] The paper begins with some defini-

[1] Cf. the letters to Locke from W. Molyneux, 27 Aug. and 22 Dec. 1692, printed in Locke's *Works* in the section 'Some Familiar Letters between Mr. Locke and several of his Friends'. Locke replied expressing doubts whether he was capable of the undertaking.

[2] Another folio sheet in the same volume (Bodl. MS. Locke, c. 28, f. 141), marked by Locke 'Ethica B', also seems to be part of his attempt to prove that ethics can be demonstrated. It contains some notes on 'Happiness', 'Censure', 'Misery', 'Law', etc., but it is only fragmentary. Lord King (op. cit. pp. 306 ff.) printed two other papers, entitled 'Thus I thinke' and 'Of Ethick in General', which form a bundle of small octavo pages, in the same volume, endorsed 'Ethica'. Locke's first commonplace book, dated 1661 (Lord King, op. cit., p. 292), contains another statement of his constant

tions and axioms, stated in hedonistic terms.[1] Morality is 'the rule of man's acting for the attaining happynesse', and happiness and misery consist of pleasure and pain. Good is 'what gives or increases pleasure or takes away or diminishes pain, and Evill is the contrary'. Locke then seeks to show that as man did not make himself or any other man, nor the world which he found made at his birth, no man has more right to anything in the world than anyone else has. Men must therefore either enjoy all things in common or determine their separate rights by compact. If things were left to be enjoyed in common, the result would be 'want, rapine and force', which would make happiness impossible. Therefore men must determine their rights by compact. Unless compacts are to be kept they are meaningless, and so 'justice is established as a duty and will be the first and generall rule of our happynesse'. To the objection, why should a man not break his word if he can thereby increase his happiness, Locke replies that as all alike are under the same rule, what is permitted to one must be permitted to all, and if everyone were allowed to break his word when it suited him the whole purpose of compacts would be frustrated. 'Justice the greatest and difficultest duty being thus established', Locke concludes, 'the rest will not be hard. The next sort of virtues are those which relate to society and soe border on justice but yet are not comprised under direct articles of contract, such as are civility, charity, liberality.'

belief that virtue 'in its obligation . . . is the will of God, discovered by natural reason, and thus far has the force of law'. . . .

[1] Cf. also the hedonism in *Essay*, II. xx. 2. Locke's ethics had always contained this element of hedonism. In 'Thus I thinke' (see previous note) he declared that 'it is a man's proper business to seek happiness and avoid misery', and in 'Of Ethick in General' that 'happiness and misery are the two great springs of human actions, and through the different ways we find men so busy in the world, they all aim at happiness, and desire to avoid misery'. But the way to get happiness was to obey the will of God.

The argument in this paper is an interesting attempt to show that the duty of justice (which apparently means keeping one's promises) can be logically inferred from the initial definitions and axioms, but it obviously contains more than an analysis of the internal agreement or disagreement of ideas, such as those of property and injustice, which was the basis of his contention that ethics were as demonstrable as mathematics. It implies, for example, knowledge, which can only be empirical, of the way men would treat each other if they were not restrained by compacts. The critic might also ask what grounds Locke had for the hedonistic theory his axioms contained. Many moralists would repudiate it and propound a quite different basis for morality, and we are thus thrown back once more on the ultimate difficulty that the attempt to establish any fundamental and indisputable grounds of morality, apart from the purely analytical agreements or disagreements which reason can perceive between various ideas, will inevitably be dogmatic. Locke warns us against the danger of 'principles taken up without questioning or examination; especially if they be such as concern morality'. According to his philosophy, 'the knowledge of the certainty of principles, as well as of other truths, depends only upon the perception we have of the agreement or disagreement of our ideas', and 'the way to improve our knowledge' is not, therefore, 'blindly, and with an implicit faith, to receive and swallow principles'.[1] This is no doubt why Locke thought that morals could be demonstrated by a logical argument from the consistency or inconsistency of ideas, but our conclusion may be that his belief in moral law was in reality more dogmatic and less ratiocinative than he maintained. Though admittedly unorthodox, he was, in fact, a Christian, and his rationalism was never as

[1] *Essay*, IV. xii. 4–6.

thorough-going as it purported to be. The God of Christianity was the unquestioned ultimate presupposition of all his thought, and the faculty of reason really operated within a sphere conditioned by his religious faith.

It was this that sustained his belief in an ultimate moral law, or law of nature. The certainty of this is not really, as he tried to maintain, a question of mathematical demonstrability, but a matter of faith. It is part of the nature of God, and of the world that he created. It is a law of reason, and is recognizable by reason, because God himself is reasonable, and reason is a faculty given to man by God as a means of recognizing his will. Granted this faith, the whole structure hangs together. But if you go behind it, and try to establish it on purely rational grounds alone, you get into difficulties. Locke retained an unshaken belief in the certainty of a moral law, as is abundantly clear in the *Second Treatise of Government*; and in the *Essay* also there can be no doubt that he rejected the view of Archelaus (and of Hobbes) that 'right and wrong, honest and dishonest, are defined only by laws and not by nature'. The law of nature is not something merely man-made or conventional, but 'we are under obligations antecedent to all human constitutions'.[1] The law of nature plays a relatively minor part in the *Essay*, whereas it permeates and is constantly referred to in the *Treatise*, but Locke's standpoint remains substantially the same in both works, and an earlier statement of the same view can be found in an entry in his Journal for 25 February 1676, headed *Obligation of Penal Laws*. Here he distinguished between 'virtues and vices antecedent to and abstract from society, as love of God, unnatural lust', and 'other virtues and vices . . . which suppose society and laws, as obedience to magistrates, or dispossessing a man of his heritage'. But even

[1] Ibid. IV. xii. 4.

with the latter he held that 'the rule and obligation is antecedent to human laws, though the matter about which that rule is may be consequent to them, as property in land, distinction, and power of persons'.[1]

Locke has been charged with inconsistency because in his *Essay* he attacked the doctrine of innate ideas, and contended that all knowledge is derived from experience, whereas he built his *Treatise* on two concepts, the state of nature and the law of nature, neither of which can be arrived at from experience, nor are they abstractions from experience in the sense which Locke gave to abstraction in the *Essay*.[2] If the law of nature is not an innate law, in order to be consistent he should have shown how our idea of it can be attributed to experience, but on the face of it he failed to do so. In the *Treatise* he does not explain how man comes to know the law of nature, but in the *Essay* he affirms that it is 'knowable by the light of nature', by which, he explains, he means 'without the help of positive revelation': it is 'something that we, being ignorant of, may attain to the knowledge of, by the use and due application of our natural faculties'.[3]

We shall best understand what Locke meant by this if we turn to a set of essays, long unpublished and unknown,

[1] Printed in Lord King, op. cit., p. 61. 'All things not commanded or forbidden by the Law of God', he continued, 'are indifferent [on which cf. below, pp. 200–1] . . . and so no human law can lay any obligation on the conscience, and therefore all human laws are purely penal, i.e. have no other obligation but to make the transgressors liable to punishment in this life. All divine laws oblige the conscience, i.e. render the transgressors liable to answer at God's tribunal, and receive punishment at his hands.' Very often both obligations coincide.

[2] Sir James Fitzjames Stephen, *Horae sabbaticae*, 2nd series (1892), ix. 150.

[3] *Essay*, I. iii. 13. The phrase 'light of nature' was well established long before Locke's time. The earliest quotation (1599) in the *O.E.D.* (*light*, 6 b) is from Thomas Cartwright: 'The light of nature teacheth some knowledge natural which is necessary to salvation', and the phrase was also used in 1630 by Prynne.

written in Latin as answers to a series of questions on the law of nature, and dating from the years between 1660 and 1664.[1] The Latin text, with a translation and summary, has been published by Dr. W. von Leyden,[2] who in his Introduction explains the circumstances in which Locke composed them. Locke, who held the office of Censor of Moral Philosophy at Christ Church in 1664,[3] gave lectures on the subject of natural law, and not long before this he had become involved in discussions with some of his colleagues on the question, much canvassed about the time of the Restoration, of religious toleration.[4] He rejected pleas for complete freedom of conscience, and appealed to reason and natural law in support of the view that the civil magistrate might properly exercise some control over religious worship. This led him on to a more general examination of natural law, and Dr. von Leyden has shown that, among other sources, he was influenced principally in composing his essays by Robert Sanderson, Regius Professor of Divinity at Oxford and subsequently Bishop of Lincoln, and the Cambridge Platonist Nathanael Culverwel.[5] It appears from later correspondence between Locke and Tyrrell[6] that he had thought of revising and

[1] These essays are contained in a small leather-bound note-book in the Lovelace Collection (Bodl. MS. Locke f. 31), and there are also drafts of some of the essays in another note-book entitled *Lemmata* (Bodl. MS. Locke e. 6).

[2] John Locke, *Essays on the Law of Nature*, ed. W. von Leyden (Oxford, 1954).

[3] The ninth and last essay, *An secundum Naturam quisquam potest esse faelix in hac vita? Neg.*, though included in the collection, is on a different footing from the rest. After some semi-humorous opening reflections on the unhappiness of life, it consists of Locke's 'funeral oration' on laying down his office as Censor—the traditional formula was 'burying the Censor'—at the end of the year.

[4] See Study VIII, below.

[5] W. von Leyden, op. cit., pp. 21 ff., 30 ff.

[6] 6 May and 29 Aug. 1687, and 27 July 1690 (Bodl. MS. Locke c. 22).

possibly publishing these early essays, and one reason why
his published works lack any extended discussion of
natural law, in spite of its being so fundamental to his
thought, may be that his intention was to treat it separately. Part of the discussion in these early essays was, in
fact, incorporated in the *Essay concerning Human Understanding*, and we shall observe a number of points that
reappeared in later works, but it is of special interest to
notice him insisting as early as this that sensation is the
source of moral as well as of other kinds of knowledge.

In spite of repeated urgings by Tyrrell, Locke never
published his essays on the law of nature, and Dr. von
Leyden has suggested that one among several reasons for
this may have been his recognition of, and failure to solve
satisfactorily, the basic inconsistency between his early
belief in absolute moral principles and his tendency later
to think in hedonistic terms. But we must beware of
exaggerating the extent or importance of this alleged inconsistency. Locke distinguished between the motive for
an action (which might be hedonistic), and the obligation
which made it morally right.[1] A man might be induced
to act in this way rather than that from motives of pain or
pleasure, but fundamentally Locke thought of the law of
nature as obligatory because it was the expression of God's
will. His ethics appears to be hedonistic, but his hedonism
itself is adapted to conformity with his religious faith.
'Good and evil', he tells us, 'are nothing but pleasure and
pain, or that which occasions or procures pleasures or

[1] Cf. J. W. Yolton, 'Locke on the Law of Nature', in *Philosophical Review*,
lxii (1958), p. 491; also R. Singh, 'John Locke and the Theory of Natural
Law', in *Political Studies*, ix (1961), pp. 105 ff. H. Aarsleff, 'The state of
nature and the nature of man', in J. W. Yolton (ed.), *John Locke: Problems
and Perspectives* (Cambridge, 1969), pp. 99 ff., esp. p. 122, and G. H. Moulds,
'The Right and the Good in Locke's Writings', in *The Locke Newsletter*,
no. 3 (1972), pp. 17 ff., esp. p. 23.

pain to us'; but God, the supreme lawgiver, has attached pleasures to certain actions and pains to others, by way of reward and punishment, so that 'morally good and evil . . . is the conformity or disagreement of our voluntary actions to some law, whereby good or evil is drawn on us from the will and power of the law-maker'.[1]

The first essay, of which the title is 'Is there a Rule of Morals, or Law of Nature, given to us? Yes',[2] opens with a demonstration of the existence of God, based on the argument from design, and there follow five arguments in support of the existence of this law. Among them we may note the fourth, drawn from the conditions of social life, which, Locke points out, necessitate a constitution and hence an obligation, independent of human will, to keep compacts;[3] and the fifth, in which he argues that apart from a natural law there would be neither virtue and vice nor reward and punishment, except what the human will itself might find in accordance with purely hedonistic or utilitarian principles.[4]

In the second essay Locke asks whether the law of nature can be known by the light of nature, and replies in the affirmative.[5] Apart from divine revelation, there are three ways of knowledge, *inscriptio*, *traditio*, and *sensus*. He does not include the faculty of reason among these, because though it handles the knowledge a man possesses, it is not itself a channel by which knowledge enters the mind. Locke postpones the question of *inscriptio*—innate knowledge—to the next (the third) essay, and passes to *traditio*. This also is not a primary source of knowledge, though the precepts of the law of nature may be handed on by means

---

[1] *Essay*, II. xxviii. 5.
[2] *An detur Morum Regula sive Lex Naturae? Affirmatur.*
[3] Cf. above, p. 9. [4] Cf. above, p. 11.
[5] *An Lex Naturae sit lumine naturae cognoscibilis? Aff.*

of it, as also by education; for one can ask how the first author of a tradition obtained his knowledge. Faith rather than knowledge is based on tradition; moreover, traditions may differ and conflict. Sense-perception thus remains the only means by which knowledge of natural law is obtained. The third essay[1] consists of arguments against the law of nature being innate: if it were, it should be universally acknowledged if not universally obeyed, but in fact it is neither. Locke accordingly propounds the view that the mind, before it receives impressions from sensation, is a *tabula rasa*.

In the fourth essay we reach the question whether reason comes to know the law of nature through sense-perception,[2] and here we learn what he means by the light of nature (*lumen naturale*);[3] it is, in effect, a combination of the inter-dependent faculties of sense-perception and reason. He explained in the second essay that by the light of nature he did not mean any inner light, placed in men by nature to teach them their duty and lead them constantly and without error in the right path. The law of nature is not innate; what is knowable by the light of nature is the kind of truth at which a man may arrive, by himself and without extraneous help, through the right use of the faculties with which he was endowed by nature. Since the light of nature, he now proceeds, is neither tradition nor any practical principle inscribed by nature in our minds, there remain only reason and sensation to account for it. These two faculties alone instruct and teach a man, and perform

[1] In answer to the fourth question, *An Lex Naturae hominum animis inscribatur? Neg.* The third question is whether the law of nature is known to us by tradition, and the reply is in the negative; but there is no essay to correspond with this title, as the subject has already been dealt with in the second essay.

[2] *An ratio per res a sensibus haustas pervenire potest in cognitionem Legis Naturae? Aff.*

[3] Cf. *Essay*, I. iii. 13, quoted above, p. 12.

what is appropriate to light: that is, they present to the mind things otherwise unknown and lying in darkness, so that they can be known and, as it were, perceived. These two faculties mutually assist each other. Sensation furnishes reason with ideas of particular sensible things, and supplies the material of discourse, while reason directs sensation, arranges among themselves the images of things derived from sensation, and forms new images from them. Neither faculty is fully effective by itself. Without reason we could scarcely attain to the level of the brutes, for various animals have senses far more acute than men's; on the other hand, reason without sensation could achieve no more than a workman in a room with closed windows and in darkness. Natural law is known by the light of nature, because it is this collaboration of the senses and reason which leads us to knowledge of the existence of an omnipotent and wise First Cause, who created the world, and whose will is concerned with human actions. The various proofs of the existence of God are all based on these faculties of sense-perception and reason, with which every human being is endowed, and it is from them alone that the knowledge of God, and of natural law which is his will, can be derived.

The fifth essay shows that the law of nature cannot be known *ex hominum consensu*.[1] *Consensus* can be positive, in which case it is based on compact, not on a principle of nature. Thus, for example, the special safety accorded by agreement to envoys is not natural. By the law of nature all men are friends, and even if they were at war in the state of nature, there is no reason in nature why envoys

[1] There is no essay corresponding to the sixth title, which asks whether the law of nature can be known from man's natural inclination (*ex inclinatione hominum naturali*), to which the answer is in the negative. In the draft version (again with no essay to correspond) the title is *An firma animi persuasio probat Legem Naturae?*

should have special treatment. This kind of *consensus* is not commanded by natural law but arises only from reasons of utility. On the other hand there may be *consensus naturalis*, i.e. agreement by natural instinct, but this will not give natural law. There never has been any universal agreement among men about moral behaviour, and even if there were it would not establish natural law. History, in fact, records many agreements to act wickedly, and the saying *Vox populi vox Dei* is false.

The sixth subject is the binding force of the law of nature,[1] and the essay opens with a reply to Hobbes's view that all natural law is directed to self-preservation. If so, Locke points out, its motive force will be not virtue but utility. Government and order in society depend on natural law, which is the source of all the obligations involved in them, and the author of natural law is God, who made it a rule for man's life. Thus all obligation, whether of natural or of positive law, is directly or indirectly attributable to God's will. In the seventh essay Locke maintained that natural law is perpetual and universal,[2] though it can assume different forms. It binds all to whom it is given: that is, all men except children and fools, who are excepted because, as they have no means of knowing it, it is not given to them.

The eighth essay denies the theory that *privata cuiusque utilitas* is the basis of the law of nature, and concludes with the assertion that the rightness of an action does not depend on its utility, but its utility is a consequence of its rightness. At the conclusion Locke signed the essay *Sic cogitavit J. Locke, 1664*. The attitude here taken up is note-

---

[1] *An Lex Naturae homines obligat? Aff.*

[2] There is no essay to correspond with the ninth title: *An Lex Naturae obligat bruta? Neg.* The idea that *ius naturale* is common to all living creatures, birds, beasts, and fishes, as well as men, is to be found in the *Digest*, but was rejected by later lawyers; cf. Pufendorf, *De Jure Naturae et Gentium*, ii. iii. 2.

worthy in its contrast with the hedonistic view expressed in the *Essay concerning Human Understanding*; but, as we saw above, Locke's was a modified hedonism, and he could have sought a reconciliation by maintaining that men should not act in certain ways simply in order to obtain the pleasure and avoid the pain which are God's rewards and punishments. Pleasure and pain may be the consequences of, and the means by which we recognize, good or bad actions, but they are not the reasons for the good man's conduct.

Locke was not really a thorough-going rationalist, any more than he was a thorough-going hedonist. Looked at purely rationally, his argument may seem to form a closed circle; but he would not find it closed, because the existence of God was to him a certainty which could be proved by reason. If his proofs do not convince us, we may say that it was faith and not reason that really provided the escape from the circle; but granted the presuppositions of that faith, the whole hung together without inconsistency. It was a question allied to this that was ultimately at stake in Locke's celebrated controversy with Stillingfleet, the Bishop of Worcester, which turned on the question whether we can have a knowledge of God and of theology purely by experience derived from sense. Locke maintained that the truths of Christianity were in consonance with reason, and could be upheld on purely rational grounds, and in 1695 he published a treatise entitled *The Reasonableness of Christianity*. Now Locke was not a Deist, and he did not mean to deny the importance for Christianity of revelation. He undoubtedly had some points in common with the Deists, but he differed from them in this. His religion was more than a merely 'natural religion', which is entirely accessible to reason; but he held that revelation never contradicts reason. The question, which should be preferred, in case revelation and reason did conflict, does not, indeed cannot, arise for him, any more than the question whether what God commands would be the law of nature even if his commands were unreasonable. For Locke, God's commands are never unreasonable, and revelation never conflicts with reason, for such is the nature of God.

We may turn to the *Second Treatise of Government* to discover the actual content of the law of nature. It is remarkably varied, and at first sight not entirely consistent either in itself or with the doctrine of the *Essay concerning Human Understanding*. Though Locke denies that the law of nature is innate, or *inscripta*, yet in support of the principle that in the state of nature every man could execute the law of nature he cites the example of Cain, who after murdering his brother cried out: *'Every one that findeth me shall slay me*; so plain was it writ in the hearts of Mankind.'[1] This and other considerations have led Mr. Peter Laslett to query whether we ought to regard Locke's *Treatises of Government* and his *Essay concerning Human Understanding* as in any way philosophically complementary. On the contrary, he argues, Locke was 'perfectly willing, indeed very anxious, that they should be seen apart', and suggests that Locke's uncomfortable awareness of his failure to solve the epistemological inconsistency between the two works may have been one reason why he so persistently refused to acknowledge his authorship of the *Two Treatises*.[2] On the other hand, Professor Aarsleff maintains that there is no conflict between the *Essay* and the *Second Treatise*. By the phrase 'writ in their hearts' (itself a biblical phrase, from Romans ii. 15), Locke only meant the same as 'known by the light of nature', and it should not be cited as evidence that he was reverting to the idea that the law

---

[1] *Second Treatise*, § 11.

[2] *Two Treatises of Government*, ed. P. Laslett (Cambridge, 1960), pp. 81 ff.

of nature is innate.[1] Locke's language was careless, but surely this is right.

Although Locke declines 'to enter...into the particulars of the Law of Nature',[2] and never expressly defines what he intends to include in it, the *Second Treatise* contains numerous passages from which we may gather various details about its content. In the first place, it is a law of equality. There are no privileges in the state of nature, which is a state of 'perfect freedom' for men 'to order their actions and dispose of their possessions and persons as they think fit, within the bounds of the law of nature'.[3] The law of nature 'willeth the preservation of all mankind', and teaches us that 'all being equal and independent, no one ought to harm another in his life, liberty, health or possessions'.[4] It might seem, then, that the law of nature embodies the principle of individual natural rights; and in one place Locke goes so far as to declare that 'natural reason' tells us that 'men being once born have a right to their preservation, and consequently to meat and drink and such other things as nature affords for their subsistence'.[5] What kind of a right is this, and how does it differ from the right Hobbes said every man has to everything, 'even to one another's body'?[6] And if men have it from birth, why are not tigers, or locusts, or the bacteria of diseases, or beef-cattle, similarly endowed with natural rights? Locke would presumably reply that the law of nature is a law of reason, and so confined to those endowed with reason.[7] Even so, how does this constitute a title to food and drink? Locke's view is, in fact, just the old scriptural (and Aristotelian)

---

[1] In J. W. Yolton (ed.), *John Locke: Problems and Perspectives* (Cambridge, 1969), p. 130.   [2] *Second Treatise*, § 12.
[3] § 4.   [4] § 6.   [5] § 25.
[6] *Leviathan*, c. xiv.
[7] Cf. p. 16, n. 1 above, and see *Second Treatise*, § 16. Cf. also below, pp. 24, 36.

doctrine that the earth, with 'all the fruits it naturally produces, and beasts it feeds', were provided by God, like reason itself, for the benefit of mankind.[1] Natural law and natural rights, therefore, are confined to men. This is not the last of our difficulties, however. A man's right to preservation might be defended if it were meant in the negative sense that murder or injury are wrong; but is a man deprived of his 'rights' if he has the misfortune to be killed in an accident, or to die in a famine?

It would, however, be unfair to Locke to insist too much on the implications of this passage, which he introduces chiefly as a preface to his discussion of property. If we read farther, we shall, I think, find that, in spite of this and similar passages,[2] Locke interprets the law of nature more socially, and less individually, than is sometimes supposed. He tells us, for example, that by the law of nature, which is common to all men, a man 'and all the rest of mankind are of one community, make up one society, distinct from all other creatures';[3] and if it were not for 'the corruption and viciousness of degenerate men' there would be no need to combine by agreements into smaller separate associations. So 'the first and fundamental natural law . . . is the preservation of the society, and (as far as will consist with the public good) of every person in it'.[4] Now this is obviously not necessarily a principle of self-interest at all, and if we return to the apparently individualist passages we shall find that they are qualifiedly so. Thus while everyone 'is bound to preserve himself', yet apparently he

---

[1] *Second Treatise*, § 26.

[2] Passages with apparently individualist implications occur mainly near the beginning of the *Second Treatise*. It is true that Locke returns to the 'fundamental, sacred and unalterable law of self-preservation' in § 149; but this appears in § 182 as 'the preservation of all mankind as much as possible', and need not be interpreted individualistically.

[3] § 128.   [4] § 134.

may not try to better himself, for he is not 'to quit his station wilfully'. A man's obligation towards others, more-over, is not merely to abstain from injuring them; it is 'by the like reason' (why?) a positive duty 'as much as he can to preserve the rest of mankind', though such altruism will only be expected, it seems, 'when his own preservation comes not in competition'.[1] Locke also tells us that 'by the fundamental law of nature, men being to be preserved as much as possible, when all cannot be preserved, the safety of the innocent is to be preferred':[2] violent men who ignore the law of nature and make war on the righteous may be destroyed like beasts of prey, because like them 'they are not under the ties of the common law of reason'. In the state of nature, the executive power of the law of nature is in every man's hand, and the law of nature consequently empowers every man to punish those who offend against it. This extends to the penalty of death, by the terms of 'that great law of nature: "Whoso sheddeth man's blood, by man shall his blood be shed".'[3] It also includes lesser penalties, proportioned in severity, for lesser offences, and it is certain, Locke declares, that such a law exists and that it is 'as intelligible and plain to a rational creature . . . as the positive laws of commonwealths; nay, possibly plainer'.[4]

Besides laying down penalties for wrongdoing, the law of nature also enjoins truth and the keeping of faith,[5] and the obligations of this 'eternal law' are 'so great and so strong in the case of promises that omnipotency itself can be tied by them. Grants, promises, and oaths are bonds that hold the Almighty.'[6] There is no obligation, however,

[1] § 6.   [2] § 16.   [3] § 11.
[4] § 12. One reason why the law of nature, though 'plain and intelligible to all rational creatures', is often broken, is that men 'being biased by their interest, as well as ignorant for want of study of it', are apt to make exceptions in their own cases (§ 124).
[5] § 14.   [6] § 195.

to keep promises extorted by force.[1] By the law of nature, again, 'Adam and Eve, and after them all parents, were . . . under an obligation to preserve, nourish, and educate' their children,[2] and in return children 'by the law of God and nature' should pay honour to their parents.[3] New-born children, however, are not under the law of nature, for 'nobody can be under a law which is not promulgated to him; and this law being promulgated or made known by reason only, he that is not come to the use of his reason cannot be said to be under this law'.[4]

In the state of nature, further, no man has 'arbitrary power over the life, liberty, or possessions of another', and this limits the powers which can be conferred on and exercised by governments:[5] yet, we learn with some astonishment, 'captives taken in a just war' are the slaves of their captors, and 'by the right of nature subjected to the absolute dominion and arbitrary power of their masters'.[6] Another 'native right' is 'to have such a legislative over them as the majority should approve and freely acquiesce in',[7] though elsewhere Locke bases the rule of majorities not on natural right but on mechanical necessity and the utilitarian argument that without it societies would dis-integrate.[8] The right of the people 'to judge whether they have just cause to make their appeal to heaven' (i.e. to launch a revolution) also belongs to them 'by a law ante-cedent and paramount to all positive laws of men'.[9] The law of nature gives some remarkably precise directions in the sphere of property rights: thus, by the 'original law of nature' anything which is removed by labour from the common state in which nature left it becomes private pro-perty: it is 'this law of reason' that 'makes the deer the Indian's who hath killed it'.[10] And the same law of nature

---

[1] *Second Treatise*, § 186.   [2] § 56.   [3] § 66.   [4] § 57.   [5] § 135.
[6] § 85.   [7] § 176.   [8] §§ 95–8.   [9] § 168.   [10] § 30.

not only gives us property but bounds it also: 'as much as any one can make use of to any advantage of life before it spoils, so much he may by his labour fix a property in'.[1] A full discussion of this topic, however, is best reserved to my study on property.

Not all these deliverances of the law of nature are consistent. The duty to keep promises, for example, obviously might conflict with a man's duty to preserve himself, or to preserve mankind, and we have noticed above how Locke shifts in his interpretation of the fundamental law that men are to be preserved, in one place putting the individual's private claim above the community's, and later sacrificing the individual to the 'public good'. Here too, however, as generally with Locke, we shall miss the point if we insist too much on verbal *minutiae*. Taking Locke's account of the law of nature as a whole, it has a general coherence, and is, at least, not repugnant to reasonable common sense. It is, in fact, more positive than this, and might not unfairly be described as roughly equivalent to the moral duties normally expected of a Protestant Christian in the seventeenth century. To a great extent, the source of Locke's inspiration on the subject of natural law was the Bible, which he cites freely. His doctrine about property, for example, is supported at various points by quotations from both Old and New Testaments. So also it was probably the Book of Genesis that suggested the notion that in the state of nature every man could execute the law of nature, in support of which he cited the example of Cain.

In view of what we have seen above this is not a surprising or an inappropriate conclusion. Moreover, Locke's whole political theory is stated in general and abstract terms, but the concrete reality lying behind it is the constitutional practice of the England of his day. The law of

[1] § 31.

nature is for him, essentially, the moral standard to which all men, including governors themselves, should conform,[1] and his insistence on it is the foundation of his case for limited, constitutional government, instead of the arbitrary power so dreaded and hated by contemporary Englishmen. It is the essential point on which his theory challenged that of Hobbes, to whom no law was real but the positive enactment of a sovereign legislative power. Locke stated this, like the rest of his theory, in terms of the philosophical tradition he inherited, but it is in accord with his practical outlook and his religious beliefs that its real meaning for him should be the dictates of the conscience of contemporary Protestantism.

[1] This principle is definitely stated in § 195: 'I will not dispute . . . whether princes are exempt from the laws of their country, but this I am sure, they owe subjection to the laws of God and nature.' In his Journal for 1681 (in the Lovelace Collection, MS. Locke f. 5, p. 86) Locke transcribed some excerpts from Hooker which summarized the view he adopted himself. 'The law of reason or human nature is that which men by discourse of natural reason have rightly found out themselves, to be all for ever bound unto in their actions'. It is 'commonly called the law of nature, and comprehendeth all those things which men by the light of their natural understanding evidently know, or at least wise may know, to be beseeming or unbeseeming, virtuous or vicious, good or evil, for them to do it'. He concluded: 'The observation of the laws of one country *officium civile*, the breach of a penal law *crimen* or *delictum*. The observation of what in any country is thought enjoined by the law of nature *virtus*, the contrary *vitium*. The observation or omission ['neglect' scratched out] of what is in credit and esteem anywhere *laus* and *vituperium*. *Licitum* is what is not forbidden or commanded by the laws of the society. *Indifferens* what is so by all the other laws. J.L.'

II

THE RIGHTS OF THE INDIVIDUAL

THE commonly accepted interpretation of Locke as a typical individualist[1] was challenged some years ago in a fresh and vigorous study of his political thought by Professor Willmoore Kendall, of the University of Illinois.[2] It is often said that Locke thought of mankind as consisting essentially of a mass of individuals endowed with natural rights. These individuals combined by compact to establish civil societies, in which the government was not to be sovereign, but was to exercise powers strictly limited by the obligation to respect the natural rights of individuals. Passages can be quoted from the *Second Treatise of Government* in support of this interpretation, but Mr. Kendall contended that it does not really represent Locke's central position. On the contrary, he argued with considerable force and subtlety that, so far from safeguarding the rights of individuals, Locke sets up a government which demands their entire obedience, and cannot be removed unless conditions become so bad that a majority of the people are driven to revolt. Mr. Kendall even went so far as to say that it is Locke, rather than Rousseau, who is really the progenitor of the 'metaphysical theory of the state'.

Not all these points were new. T. H. Green, for example,

[1] Professor C. E. Vaughan, for example, laid particular stress on Locke's individualism (*Studies in the History of Political Philosophy before and after Rousseau*, Manchester, 1925, i. 130 ff.).

[2] Willmoore Kendall, 'John Locke and the Doctrine of Majority-Rule' (*Illinois Studies in the Social Sciences*, xxvi, no. 2, 1941).

remarked that the essential ideas of Rousseau are to be found in Locke's *Treatise*,[1] and many critics have noticed features of Locke's theory which seem inconsistent with the usual individualist interpretation of him. The critics have varied, however, in the degree of emphasis they have laid on such discrepancies, and have generally tended to treat the individualism as fundamental, and to minimize what is inconsistent with this, either ignoring it in their final verdict or dismissing it as ill-considered and unrepresentative of Locke's real view. Mr. Kendall, in effect, reverses this tendency. It is the individualist passages which are inconsistencies for him,[2] and he emphasizes instead the points—and they certainly amount to a considerable array —on the other side. I believe he goes too far, and I would even say that I believe he is quite wrong in his general summing-up of Locke's intention and significance. Nevertheless, his revaluation, if sometimes perverse, is clever and stimulating, and has given a salutary stir to the study of Locke. I propose in this study to consider briefly some of Mr. Kendall's arguments, in the hope of arriving at some more definitive conclusion.

Locke's theory is commonly held to begin with an account of men in the state of nature. On the contrary, says Mr. Kendall, Locke begins with an authoritarian and collectivist definition of political power, and subsequently puts men into a state of nature in order to provide himself with a standpoint from which to survey societies under government. It is true that Locke's Chapter II, 'Of the State of Nature', is preceded by his well-known definition of political power, which forms the end of his introductory

---

[1] *Principles of Political Obligation*, § 51.

[2] *Second Treatise*, § 168, for example, where the liberty to revolt is said to come into play if even 'any single man' is deprived of his right, is 'Locke at his most reckless'.

first chapter.[1] Its place there, however, is as much to conclude the transition effected in this chapter from the *First
Treatise* as to provide a definition by which political is to
be distinguished from other kinds of power,[2] and I doubt
if much importance should be attached to its place in the
Second Treatise. Whether it is an authoritarian and collectivist definition or not will depend on what is meant by
'collectivist', and the extent to which political power is
limited in practice by being confined to the pursuit of the
'public good'. This is a crucial phrase in Locke's theory, to
which we shall have to return later.

There is more substance (but nothing novel) in Mr.
Kendall's next point, that men in the state of nature are
not discrete individuals but highly socialized, and that
their rights are rights originating in social needs. It is
obvious enough that if men in the state of nature are subject to the law of nature and have rights and duties, the
state of nature is itself social. Locke himself expressly says
that by the law of nature a man 'and all the rest of mankind are of one community, make up one society, distinct
from all other creatures'.[3] Elsewhere, however, he pictures
the state of nature and its obligations as subsisting between
isolated men 'in the woods of America', and remarks that
'truth and keeping of faith belong to men as men, and not
as members of society'.[4] These passages must be read in
their contexts. In the one he is expressly emphasizing the
social characteristics of humanity, and arguing that the
deliberate creation of separate political units would be
unnecessary were it not for the wickedness of some men;

---

[1] 'A right of making laws with penalties of death, and consequently all less
penalties, for the regulating and preserving of property, and of employing
the force of the community in the execution of such laws, and in the defence
of the commonwealth from foreign injury, and all this only for the public
good' (§ 3).

[2] *Second Treatise*, § 2.   [3] § 128.   [4] § 14.

the other is a reply to sceptics who doubted the existence
of a state of nature, in which he tells them that it exists
between any men who are not subject to a common government. To be exact he should have said that keeping of faith
belongs to men as men and not as members of *political*
society; apart from this there is no real inconsistency,
and Locke's underlying point is the same in both passages
—the reality and validity of the obligations of the law of
nature. It is certainly unfair to accuse Locke of treating
society as an artifact pieced together by imaginary individuals. His civil society may be artificial, but his state
of nature is itself social, and what he emphasizes is not so
much the isolation of individuals as the importance of the
family and the dependence of children on their parents.
Mr. Kendall's main point, however, is that Locke's state
of nature is really only an expository device and not an
historical fact, even though he may pretend that it is.

One of the characteristics of Locke's state of nature is
the existence in it of natural rights, but according to Mr.
Kendall these rights, including the right of property in
which they centre, are not individualist. The law of nature
(1) 'willeth the preservation of all mankind', and God (2)
gave the world to men 'in common'. It is true that
everyone (3) has a private property in his own body, but
the right of property in what a man has mixed his labour
with is deduced, Mr. Kendall suggests, not from this last
alone, but from all three premisses together. Moreover, a
man is not entitled to more property than he can use:
anything he appropriates above this limit is 'more than
his share and belongs to others'. The right of property, in
fact, is not so much a right belonging to individuals as a
function of men's duty to enrich the common heritage.
I discuss Locke's theory of property more fully in a separate study, and will therefore leave it here and pass on to

Mr. Kendall's next point, which is that the rights which exist within organized society are not the inalienable rights of individuals, but are always created by the law, which wills the good of the whole. Thus, it is necessary and just that all the members of a political community should sacrifice some of their natural liberty, because the 'many conveniences' they are to enjoy as citizens arise 'from the labour, assistance, and society of others in the same community'.[1]

Now, are the 'many conveniences' of citizenship all the rights a citizen has, or does he carry natural rights over into the state (in accordance with the more usual interpretation), and enjoy them there under the protection of government instead of subject to the risks and 'inconveniences' of the state of nature? In the state of nature, according to Locke, apart from 'the liberty he has of innocent delights', a man has two powers: first, 'to do whatsoever he thinks fit for the preservation of himself and others within the permission of the law of nature',[2] and second, the power personally to punish breaches of that law. This second power he gives up wholly, and 'engages his natural force . . . to assist the executive power of the society, as the law thereof shall require'.[3] The first power 'he gives up to be regulated by laws made by the society, so far forth as the preservation of himself and the rest of that society shall require'. These laws 'in many things confine the liberty he had by the law of nature',[4] but Locke must have meant that some part of it is retained. In the next paragraph he tells us that the citizen 'has to part with as much of his natural liberty . . . as the good, prosperity,

---

[1] *Second Treatise*, § 130.   [2] § 128.
[3] § 130. Cf. § 89, where the total surrender of this power is said to be the distinguishing mark of a political, or civil, society.
[4] § 129.

and safety of the society shall require'.[1] He does not tell us how much this is, but the common assumption is that a citizen at any rate retains his natural right of property entire:[2] he cannot be made to part with his property (whether by taxation or otherwise) without his consent.[3] According to a previous chapter, what has to be surrendered is 'all the power necessary to the ends for which they unite into society',[4] but Locke varies somewhat in his treatment of this question, for later on he tells us that men 'give up all their natural power to the society which they enter into', though the chief purpose of this sacrifice is 'that they may have the united strength of the whole society to secure and defend their properties'.[5] On the whole, then, I should dispute Mr. Kendall's contention that Locke thought of all rights in the state as created by the law, if by this he means the positive law of the state. I should agree, however, that he thought of rights as held subject to, and possibly as created by, natural law.

Did Locke mean his state of nature to be taken as an historical fact, or is it, as Mr. Kendall maintains, only an expository device? It is true that much of Locke's most individualist language is connected with the state of nature. It is at the supposed inauguration of the state by the social compact that unanimity is required[6] (whereas after that the decision of a majority is binding), so that if

[1] *Second Treatise*, § 130.

[2] Cf. § 124: 'The great and chief end . . . of men's uniting into commonwealths, and putting themselves under government, is the preservation of their property.'

[3] § 138. But cf. also §§ 120 and 140, and see pp. 75, 101 below, for a discussion of what consent means here.

[4] § 99.

[5] § 136.

[6] Cf. § 96: 'that which acts any community being only the consent of the individuals of it', and a few lines farther down, 'the consent of every individual that united into it'. I discuss this topic more fully in the next study.

this can be dismissed as imaginary, and we need only consider the relation between the subjects of governments already established, much of Locke's apparent individualism may disappear. Now, to many writers of the seventeenth and eighteenth centuries the state of nature and the social contract were, I think, admittedly only expository devices, and were never thought of as having actually occurred. This is certainly the case with Hobbes, and also with Rousseau. With Locke, however, I am not so sure. My impression is that the Whigs of the Revolution of 1688 believed their original contract to have been historical, though they hedged when the Tories challenged them on this point. This, of course, was a contract between king and people, and not, like Locke's, a compact to establish a government, but I am inclined to think that Locke, too, believed in the historicity of his compact. In reply to critics who disputed this, he pleads that records do not take us back beyond the institution of governments, and he cites an account of the situation in Peru and other parts of America, together with the case of 'those who went away from Sparta with Palantus', as examples of the actual establishment of governments by the consent of free individuals. He is aware that nothing is easier or more natural than for a father's control over his family to grow into the political authority of monarchy,[1] and that governments may well have originated by a union of families;[2] but he argues that where the father's power over his children is continued beyond their minority, this is only by their consent.[3] He also tries to show that, after the (real or imaginary) initial inauguration of the state, later generations who are born into it only become members of it by consent, though this consent may be given tacitly, and 'being given separately in their turns, as each comes to be

[1] *Second Treatise*, §§ 75, 76.   [2] § 112.   [3] § 74.

of age, and not in a multitude together, people take no notice of it'.[1] That this argument is weak and open to obvious objections I do not deny, and I discuss these points more fully in another study.[2] The point here, however, is that Locke meant his doctrine of individual consent seriously, and that it is not eliminated by dismissing his account of the initiation of political society, but was a fundamental assumption of his whole theory. 'Reason', he concludes, 'is plain on our side that men are naturally free',[3] and consequently nothing can 'put a man into subjection to any earthly power but only his own consent'.[4]

This assumption is the basis of his doctrine that the power of a government over aliens in its territory rests only on the law of nature. 'Those who have the supreme power of making laws in England, France, or Holland', he remarks, 'are to an Indian but like the rest of the world—men without authority.[5] This sounds strange in modern ears, but it is the logical consequence of Locke's firm belief that all governmental authority is based on consent. 'Laws, by virtue of any sanction they receive from the promulgated will of the legislative, reach not a stranger: they speak not to him, nor, if they did, is he bound to hearken to them.' Nobody would propound such a doctrine today, for we have come to recognize that the authority of government is something inherent in the nature of society, irrespective of personal consent, and covers everyone, alien and citizen, even though aliens do not owe allegiance. Locke, however, not only accepted this assumption himself, but evidently expected his readers to share his belief. It is easy to point out, as critics have often done, that in practice the political structure he describes is an inadequate safeguard of individual liberties, but this does

---

[1] *Second Treatise*, § 117.   [2] See pp. 72, 73, below.
[3] § 104.   [4] § 119.   [5] § 9.

not discredit the usual interpretation of Locke as, at least in intention, an upholder of the rights of individuals.

We have seen that Locke defined political power in terms of 'the public good'. Mr. Kendall complains that Locke does not distinguish, and indeed seems unaware of the differences between, the aggregate goods of a number of individuals, and a general good, which involves a community with sufficient cohesion to possess some common interests. When Locke wants to show the necessity of government, he writes as if men's interests diverged so much that coercion is necessary to restrain them from 'invading others' rights, and from doing hurt to one another';[1] but such circumstances almost rule out a common good. On the other hand, when he wants to show that obedience is worth while, he takes for granted enough common interest to constitute a public good. Now, if Locke were a consistent and thorough-going individualist, he should have tried to prove not only that men join a society to preserve their individual natural rights, but that their continued obedience to its government similarly promotes their individual interests. In fact he proves nothing of the kind, but upholds the legitimacy of a government which promotes the public interest. Rousseau also set out 'to find a form of association which will defend and protect with the whole common force the person and goods of each associate', but in which each 'may still obey himself alone and remain as free as before'.[2] His plan, however, was to force recalcitrants to find their real freedom in submission to the general will, which pursues, not their private interests, but 'the common interest uniting them'.[3]

If Rousseau began as an individualist, he ended as an authoritarian, and pointed the way to Hegel and the idealist school. Is Mr. Kendall right in seeing in Locke the

[1] § 7.   [2] *Contrat Social*, i. 6.   [3] Ibid. ii. 4.

real precursor of this way of thought? There are un-doubtedly phrases and sentences in Locke which may sug-gest such an interpretation. Perhaps the most striking is the passage where he tells us that 'law in its true notion is not so much the limitation as the direction of a free and intelligent agent to his proper interest,[1] and prescribes no farther than is for the general good of those under that law: . . . that ill deserves the name of confinement which hedges us in only from bogs and precipices. So that . . . the end of law is, not to abolish or restrain, but to preserve and enlarge freedom'.[2] It should be observed, however, that the law Locke is here referring to is not the positive law of any state, but the law of nature, which governed Adam as well as his posterity. His argument is that, as a man can only know and be under this law when he comes of age and can use his reason, so 'Adam's children, being not presently as soon as born under this law of reason, were not presently free'.[3] This certainly seems like a premonition of the distinctions drawn later by Rousseau and Kant be-tween natural and civil liberty, and it cannot be denied that the whole paragraph has a perceptibly collectivist tone. Similarly we may notice Locke's description of the supreme executive in the state as 'the public person vested with the power of the law, . . . to be considered as the

[1] His 'real will', may we say?

[2] *Second Treatise*, § 57. Part of this sounds like an echo of a similar passage in Hobbes, *Leviathan*, c. 30, in which good laws are compared with hedges, 'set not to stop travellers, but to keep them in their way'.

[3] Cf. his phraseology in § 59, where he writes, not of being free from the restraints imposed by law, but of a man 'under the law of nature' being 'free of that law', a condition he attains only when he is sufficiently adult to be able to exercise his reason and voluntarily conform to the law. Similarly, a man is 'free of' the law of England when he has 'the liberty to dispose of his actions and possessions according to his own will, within the permission of that law'. Cf. J. L. Stocks, *Locke's Contribution to Political Theory* (Ter-centenary Addresses, Oxford, 1933), p. 4.

image, phantom, or representative of the commonwealth, acted by the will of the society', so that a distinction can be drawn between his 'public will' and 'his own private will'.[1] But though Locke firmly believed that government and law were necessary for the preservation and indeed the enlargement of liberty, he never *identified* liberty with obedience to law. The essence of liberty was to be 'free from restraint and violence from others'. It was not, indeed, 'a liberty for every man to do what he lists: (for who could be free when every man's humour might domineer over him?)', but a man was free when he could 'dispose and order . . . his person, actions, possessions, and his whole property, within the allowance of those laws under which he is; and therein not to be subject to the arbitrary will of another, but freely to follow his own'.[2]

Another interesting point to which Mr. Kendall draws attention is Locke's rather unexpected phraseology in the passage where he declares that, in pursuance of the law of nature, 'which willeth the peace and preservation of all mankind', everyone has 'a right to punish the transgressors of that law'.[3] In the previous paragraph he says that every man ought 'as much as he can to preserve the rest of mankind', and though we might speak of an injured individual's 'right' to retaliate, we might expect the punishment of transgressors in order to 'preserve the innocent' to be called a duty rather than a right. Locke's 'sleight of hand', as Mr. Kendall calls it, with the word 'right' veils the claim which this law of nature makes on individuals in the common interest. As he observes, this is no inalienable individual right, except to perform his duty and to be treated as a man (i.e. as a member of the community of mankind) so long as he serves the common good. In society this becomes a duty to promote the 'public good' of a man's

[1] *Second Treatise*, § 151.   [2] § 57.   [3] § 7.

society, which Locke treats as equivalent to the welfare of mankind in general. Passages like this are not individualist in tone, and if we are driven to choose between these and the very definitely individualist passages noticed earlier, which shall we choose as representing Locke's real view? Or shall we just suppose that he was too careless a philosopher to notice that there was any discrepancy?

The truth surely is that for Locke such a discrepancy simply did not exist, because he did not draw a distinction between the public good and the particular goods of individuals. For him the one was the sum of the other, and though it is true that he was more concerned in some contexts with the particulars and in others with the total, he equated the public good with the preservation of the property (i.e. the lives, liberties, and estates) of individuals. He does not have to 'prove' that individuals promote their private interests best by obeying the government. As he repeatedly says, that is the purpose for which government exists. Nowadays, when the public good may be viewed in overtly 'collectivist', or indeed socialist terms, it may run counter, for example when the 'progressive' taxation of incomes or property is considered, to the private interests of property-owners. Locke never thought of a government as 'collectivist' in that sense. He thought in terms of a society and government of property-owners, whose interests would naturally coincide. And it is hardly fair of Mr. Kendall to accuse Locke of sharp practice when he treats the duty of preserving the rest of mankind as a right. A government must have the right to punish criminals in order to protect its citizens and their property, and all Locke is doing is to explain the origin of this right.

Locke's friend and correspondent James Tyrrell similarly made no distinction between the common good and the particular goods of individuals, and evidently thought that to secure the one necessarily involved securing the others too. 'By the common good of rational beings', he wrote, 'I understand the collective happiness of the Deity, as the Head of them, and that of all the individual persons of mankind, existing together with us, as the constituent parts or members, and in which each man's particular good and happiness is included, since it is impossible to endeavour the happiness of others, as voluntary agents, unless each particular person, whose duty it is so to do, have first a right to preserve and make himself happy, jointly with others in his proportion to the whole body of mankind.'[1]

We may perhaps, if we look at it from a modern 'collectivist' point of view, conclude that Locke's confidence in the identity of public and private interests was one of the most notable weaknesses of his political philosophy. According to Dr. Reinhold Niebuhr, it is a defect of liberal thought in general that it relies too much 'upon either the capacity of reason to transmute egoism into a concern for the general welfare, or upon the ability of government to overcome the potential conflict of wills in society'. A further weakness is that Locke does not seem to consider the possibility of conflict between public and private interests except on the comparatively low level of the primitive instinct of survival or 'self-preservation'. But 'most of the gigantic conflicts of will in human history, whether between individuals or groups, take place on a level where "self-preservation" is not immediately, but only indirectly involved. They are conflicts of rival lusts and ambitions.'[2] One could point to other powerful forces (the ties of nation or of race, for example) which Locke's political philosophy

[1] J. Tyrrell, *A Brief Disquisition of the Law of Nature* (1692), p. 108.
[2] Reinhold Niebuhr, *The Children of Light and the Children of Darkness* (1945), p. 25.

fails to take account of, so that it cannot help seeming inadequate as a solution of the complex and difficult problem of the relationship between the individual and society.
We must not forget, however, that when Locke wrote his
Two Treatises of Government in the latter part of the seventeenth century, he was not attempting to provide answers
to all the questions that may interest a modern political
theorist. His primary purpose was to refute the Tory political theory, based on the doctrines of Sir Robert Filmer,
which seemed to threaten a dangerous enlargement of
royal power.

   This is not to deny that Locke's theory was inadequate
in more than one respect, and inadequate not only for our
age but even for his own. This is notably the case in regard
to the question of religious toleration. One might have
expected that the prevalence of intolerance and persecution—a subject on which Locke had felt deeply for years—
would have impelled him to try and get to the roots of the
problem of the relationship between government and the
consciences of individuals. His discussion of this subject is
fuller in the *Letter on Toleration* than in the *Treatise*, but it is
still disappointingly insufficient. His reply to the question
'What if the magistrate by his decree should order something which seems unlawful to the conscience of a private
person?' is that 'if the commonwealth is governed in good
faith, and the counsels of the magistrates are really
directed to the common good of the citizens, this will
seldom happen'. Apart from this optimistic assumption
that conflict is unlikely to arise, he just evades the issue
by identifying the individual's conscience with the public
good. He goes on to remark that 'the private judgement of
any person concerning a law enacted in political matters,
for the public good, does not take away the obligation of
that law, nor does it deserve toleration'—an attitude which

logically involves a complete refusal to tolerate any conscientious objectors—and concludes finally that if the
magistrate believes his laws to be for the public good, and
his subjects persist in believing the contrary, God alone
can be judge between them. In other words, revolt is the
last resort; but here again it will be noticed that he has
dropped the case of the conscientious individual and writes
in terms of 'subjects' in the plural. The conclusion one
reaches is that Locke's phraseology is too bluntly fashioned
to be worth scrutinizing under a microscope. After all, he
did not employ carefully defined technical terms, but the
ordinary inexact language of everyday life. If the word is
worth retaining at all, I think Locke can still be called an
individualist; but he was not a thorough-going nor a
strictly consistent one.

How in fact does a government conform to Locke's re-
quirement that it must seek the public good? It must
'govern by established standing laws, promulgated and
known to the people, and not by extemporary decrees; by
indifferent and upright judges, who are to decide controversies by those laws; and to employ the force of the
community at home only in the execution of such laws, or
abroad, to prevent or redress foreign injuries, and secure
the community from inroads and invasions'.[1] Does this
mean that a government is to have only limited powers?
It is clear that Locke shared to the full the bitter hostility
felt not only by the Whigs but by most seventeenth-century
Englishmen for 'arbitrary' power. Whatever powers his
government is to exercise, they must be exercised consti-
tutionally. Mr. Kendall suggests that he has a horror of
personal authority,[2] and I think we should agree. The seventeenth century was the age of absolute monarchies, and the
arbitrary power of irresponsible monarchs like James II

[1] *Second Treatise*, § 131.   [2] Cf. §§ 17, 22, 92, 172.

was in Locke's mind a tyranny to be repudiated. Most of us would agree that Locke has no place in his system for an absolute sovereign such as that of Hobbes.[1] It has been said that Locke's argument was 'an attack directed far more against the idea of sovereignty than against the claims of absolute monarchy',[2] and Locke has been seen as one of the originators of the principle of the separation of powers, which was a device deliberately designed to prevent the accumulation of absolute power in the hands of any one branch of the government.[3] This, however, is going too far. Locke recognizes the supremacy of the legislature, and though he devotes a chapter to the question of the extent of its power,[4] the limits he sets to it are not a matter of positive law. On the other hand, government was under an unmistakable moral obligation to respect the law of nature, and to frame its legislation accordingly. 'The obligations of the law of nature cease not in society, but only in many cases are drawn closer, and have by human laws known penalties annexed to them to enforce their observation. Thus the law of nature stands as an eternal rule to all men, legislators as well as others. The rules they make for other men's actions must . . . be conformable to the law

[1] The concluding sentences of § 93 appear to be directed against Hobbes. But it has been suggested that Locke was really a Hobbist who timidly tried to conceal his real views. On this see below, p. 119.

[2] J. N. Figgis, *The Divine Right of Kings* (2nd edn., Cambridge, 1914), p. 242. C. E. Vaughan said the same (op. cit. i. 134).

[3] I discuss this question more fully in a later study (no. V), q.v.

[4] Chap. XI. It 'is not nor can possibly be absolutely arbitrary over the lives and fortunes of the people'; it 'cannot assume to itself a power to rule by extemporary decrees, but is bound to dispense justice . . . by promulgated, standing laws': it 'cannot take away from any man any part of his property without his own consent'; and fourthly it 'cannot transfer the power of making laws into any other hands', because it is 'but a delegated power from the people', and 'they who have it cannot pass it over to others'. Its laws, he further explains, are to be equal for all classes, rich and poor, 'the favourite at court and the countryman at plough'.

of nature, i.e. to the will of God, of which that is a declaration.'[1]

Locke describes the conditions under which the government (in both its legislative and executive branches) is to exercise power, as a trust, and he thus conveys the notion of responsibility for its proper exercise, and the liability to forfeiture in case of abuse. It is noticeable that in this connection he drops his individualist phraseology. It is 'the community' which entrusts the legislature with power,[2] and this power is 'limited to the public good of the society'.[3] Similarly it is 'the community' which 'perpetually retains a supreme power of saving themselves from the attempts and designs' of anybody foolish or wicked enough to plot against 'the liberties and properties of the subject'.[4] But we need not argue that in using this phraseology Locke had inconsistently forgotten his 'individualism' and become a 'collectivist'. Now that he had passed the stage at which a community had been established, it was natural for him to write in terms appropriate to that stage. The last-mentioned supreme power, which is the ultimate sanction in Locke's political system, is the famous right to 'appeal to Heaven', or in other words, the right of revolution. This is an inalienable right, which belongs to the people 'by a law antecedent and paramount to all positive laws of men'.[5]

It is here, as it seems to me, that Mr. Kendall most seriously misinterprets Locke. The basic reason why he does so, I believe, is that he insists on regarding the *Second Treatise of Government* as a purely academic treatise which sets out to solve in the abstract the general problems of

---

[1] *Second Treatise*, § 135.   [2] § 136.
[3] § 135. Cf. also the language of § 134, where the necessary authority for the validity of law is said to be 'the consent of society' (not of individuals).
[4] § 149.   [5] § 168.

political theory. Now it is true that Locke is careful to write in general terms, and indeed one of the reasons why he had such influence may well have been that he seemed to state what was really a partisan view on a controversial topic as if it were a deliverance of pure reason. The *Treatise* was published, for all that, with contemporary circumstances very much in mind, as Locke indeed clearly declares in his Preface; and in his discussion of the constitutional powers of the different branches of government, and of the manner in which the right of revolution might come into play, the English scene he is really describing is disguised with the thinnest of veils.[1]

Mr. Kendall argues that Locke's reservation to the people of an ultimate right of revolution, which is in effect an ultimate right to decide whether a government is to be retained in power or not, amounts to making the people sovereign, and the real question to be answered is, not whether the government set up by the people is limited, but whether there are any limits to this ultimate power of revolution: in particular, is it limited by any inalienable natural rights still retained in the hands of individuals? The answer, he thinks, is clear. 'The power that every individual gave the society when he entered into it, can never revert to the individuals again as long as the society lasts.'[2] This means that so long as a government's title to act for the commonwealth is beyond dispute, the rights of the individual, including his rights of property, are merely those allowed him by positive law. A man cannot dispute a law duly enacted because he thinks it violates the law of nature or his natural rights, or is not directed to peace and safety and the public good. As a member of the community he has surrendered both his right of private judgement and

[1] Occasionally (e.g. in §§ 165, 167) he drops any pretence at disguise at all.
[2] § 243.

the power to act on his convictions. Moreover, in spite of his claims for the principle of consent, Locke has put these powers, of coercing individuals and making judgements that they cannot dispute, into the hands of a majority. Not only so, but the ultimate power of judging whether there is just cause to 'appeal to Heaven' will rest with a majority. Locke defends himself against the possible charge that his theory 'lays a perpetual foundation for disorder' by urging that 'this operates not till the inconvenience is so great that the majority feel it and are weary of it'.[1]

The rights of the individual in society, accordingly, turn out to be such rights as are compatible with the 'public good', and this means, in effect, that he must pay unquestioning obedience to the will of the majority. Locke, Mr. Kendall concludes, has got away with a reputation as a liberal on the strength of some platitudes in the opening chapters of the *Treatise*, which are completely belied by the implications of his system as it develops. In reality he is an authoritarian who out-Rousseaus Rousseau.[2] Nor is this the last of Mr. Kendall's charges. Though Locke is what he calls a 'majority-rule democrat', he omits to supply any political machinery for consulting the will of the majority. The people play no part in the constitution except by intervening at occasional revolutions. A majority in the past may have set up an oligarchical government, or even an

[1] § 168. Mr. Kendall is right in thinking that this represents Locke's real view much more than his phrase, a few lines above in the same paragraph, about 'any single man' being deprived of his right. As he admits later (§ 230), 'the examples of particular injustice or oppression of here and there an unfortunate man' are likely to be ignored. The same point, that the popular right of revolution can only take effect if the majority decide to act, was noticed by M. Bion Smyrniadis, *Les Doctrines de Hobbes, Locke et Kant sur le droit d'insurrection* (Paris, 1921), pp. 181–204.

[2] This is indeed to turn the tables on Professor Vaughan, who had thought Locke's argument, 'if sound, as fatal to the ideal of Rousseau as to that of Hobbes' (op. cit. i. 134).

hereditary monarchy, which will be allowed to continue ruling indefinitely so long as it recognizes that it is a trustee and does not too flagrantly violate the public good. Locke was blind also to the risk of genuine decisions being vitiated by a 'crystallized majority' which always votes together as a group on every issue, so that a member of a minority knows in advance that he cannot affect the vote. Locke may have thought that a government should be continuously responsive to the will of the majority, but it is questionable whether the knowledge that the majority possesses an ultimate right of revolution will be an adequate guarantee of this, or whether there can be such a thing as a majority-will unless there are political institutions to give shape and expression to it. Again, a majority might fail to revolt, even when revolution would be justified, and even if it did revolt, the revolution would not necessarily succeed. Moreover, revolutions which do succeed are often the work of organized minorities, even if the majority subsequently comes to acquiesce. The real need, Mr. Kendall concludes, is for proper constitutional machinery by which the will of the people may be regularly consulted. This is where modern writers have improved on Locke.

All this seems to me singularly perverse, and, as a criticism of Locke, quite wide of the mark. Surely Mr. Kendall goes quite astray in interpreting Locke's later chapters as if they were a timeless, abstract, and general treatise on the art of government. It seems to me quite absurd to call Locke a 'majority-rule democrat' on the strength of the people's ultimate right of occasional revolution, and a misuse of a term (too often misused by many others in the past) to describe the people on that account as sovereign, more particularly considering that Locke himself avoided this word (perhaps because of its Hobbesian associations), and expressly stated that the power of the community was supreme 'not as considered under any form of government', because it could not take effect until the government was dissolved. There is no point in criticizing Locke because his book does not contain all the latest doctrines of a writer on political science. The realities behind his apparently general discussion were the English constitution of the late seventeenth century, as viewed by contemporary Whigs, and their fears that it was being endangered by the Stuart monarchy. His constitutional ideas were based on the accepted traditions and practices of the England of his time, and it is simply unhistorical to examine them and find them wanting in the light of the experience of the nineteenth and twentieth centuries. It is not a question of whether, in general, it would not be better to have demo-cratic machinery for ascertaining the will of the people rather than to rely on the chances of the successful out-come of an occasional revolution in case an existing government became intolerable. Locke was not really pro-pounding a general doctrine for common adoption. His aim was to justify the Whig programme by trying to show that it was in accord with the law of nature and the rest of the widely accepted stock-in-trade of contemporary political science.

Mr. Kendall concludes his sometimes perverse but always stimulating discussion by suggesting a key to the puzzle of how Locke could believe simultaneously in the right of the majority to enforce its will and in the supre-macy in politics of the moral standard embodied in natural law. To say 'right is what the majority wills' is not the same as to say 'the majority always wills what is right', even though they may come to the same thing as principles of practical politics. The first proposition by itself implies a relativist ethical doctrine, whereas the second involves only the quantitative judgement that the wise and just outnumber the foolish and unjust, and is not inconsistent with a belief in absolute moral standards, valid irrespective of the will of majorities. But then, as Mr. Kendall observes, the first proposition is also consistent with such a belief when it is put forward as a corollary of the second. He suggests that this was Locke's real belief, though he did not state it explicitly. He assumed that the majority of ordinary men were rational and just. Therefore he could safely put supreme power into the hands of a majority, because the majority would in practice never abuse its power. He could uphold simultaneously both the rights of individuals and the rights of a majority because the kind of majority he had in mind would always pursue what is rational and just, and the duty of the individual to obey would follow immediately from his duty to promote the rational and just.

I am doubtful whether Locke would have accepted Mr. Kendall's statement as an amplification of his unwritten thoughts, but I suspect that some of the logical difficulties which critics like Mr. Kendall, and others before him, have found in the *Treatise* arise simply because Locke did not notice them, and that he would have been surprised at the ingenuity expended in trying to reconcile them. But it is interesting to notice that the view Mr. Kendall reaches, at the end of his journey, is much the same as that suggested by the quotation from Dr. Niebuhr above. Was Locke then, after all, an individualist? I think we can say he was, but he was not a thorough-going, extreme individualist, any more than he was a thorough-going rationalist. He stands mid-way between two extreme positions in politics—on the one hand the doctrine which bases government on divine right (the most extreme form of that being Filmer's patriarchal theory), and on the other the doctrine of consent, so called, which derives the force of laws from the will of the sovereign people, and makes government the artificial product of agreement or compact. Locke's fundamental tenet was natural law, which is God's will, to which all laws and all government must conform. His position is not, however, exactly mid-way between these two extremes, but inclines somewhat towards the left. He specifically attacks Filmer and the divine right of kings, and he sympathizes with, and often, if loosely, uses, the language of consent. But government is not for him a merely artificial device. It is the natural remedy for the inconveniences of the state of nature, and man is naturally social.[1] Nor is Locke a radical, like Milton. Provided the government discharges its trust (that is, governs in accordance with natural law), it cannot be disobeyed and overthrown at pleasure. It has a right to expect obedience, and provided it governs in accordance with natural law, which is God's will, its right to govern might even, in a modified sense, be called a divine right.

Hooker, whom Locke often quoted, similarly stands in a middle position, and forms a bridge between these extreme points of view. Or rather, perhaps, he represents a point of view which comprehended the elements of truth in both extremes, and stood between them, not because he had both before him and could choose, or that he wished to compromise or reconcile them; but rather because in his time political theory had not yet hardened into a radical dichotomy between them. Professor d'Entrèves has suggested that Locke quoted some of Hooker's phrases in order to enlist his support for a more definite and uncompromisingly individualist theory that can properly be

---

[1] Cf. *Second Treatise*, § 77: 'God having made man such a creature, that in his own judgement it was not good for him to be alone, put him under strong obligations . . . to drive him into society.'

ascribed to Hooker himself.[1] I accept his judgement about Hooker; but I would go farther, for I am inclined to think that in our final summing up we should give Locke a place not so far removed from Hooker after all. Some of Locke's language, it is true, is more pronouncedly individualist than Hooker's, but he does not work out his theory in terms entirely consistent with this. He was capable of misquoting Hooker, or at any rate of quoting him in a misleading way.[2] I suspect that one of the reasons why he included so many quotations from Hooker in the *Second Treatise* was that he reckoned that Hooker would carry conviction with his Tory opponents.[3] At the same time, his note-books and commonplace-books show how deeply he had read and pondered Hooker's work, and I think he realized that he owed a philosophical debt to Hooker, and felt a definite affinity with his thought.

A somewhat similar parallel can be traced between Locke's thought and that of his French Huguenot contemporary, Pierre Jurieu. Here again a recent critic notices the resemblance, but goes on to remark that Jurieu was much less of an individualist than Locke, and contrasts the importance of religion in Jurieu's political theory with the purely secular and utilitarian rationalism which he associates with the individualism of Locke.[4] Locke's

[1] A. P. d'Entrèves, *The Medieval Contribution to Political Thought* (Oxford, 1939), pp. 125–32.

[2] Cf. p. 56, n. 1, below.

[3] The same motive evidently impelled Sir George Treby, in the debates in the Convention in 1689, to assert that the 'original contract' was 'a phrase and thing used by the learned Mr. Hooker, . . . whom I mention as a valuable authority, being one of the best men, the best churchman, and the most learned of our nation in his time, and his works are very worthily recommended by the testimony of King Charles I. He alloweth, that government did originally begin by Compact and Agreement' (*Parly. Hist.* v. 79).

[4] G. H. Dodge, *The Political Theory of the Huguenots of the Dispersion* (New York, 1947), pp. 64, 65.

thought certainly contains some elements which suggest an anticipation of utilitarianism, but to call his outlook secular is surely a serious misunderstanding. The truth is, I think, that both in this respect and in the character of his individualism Locke stands closer to Jurieu, as well as to Hooker, than has been supposed. We may conclude, then, that Locke was an individualist in a qualified sense. He did not imagine the state to be an artificially fabricated combination of naturally separate individuals; he did not champion the individual against the community, and barely considered the possibility of conflict between them. But the government he recommended was in effect the parliamentary limited monarchy approved of by his Whig contemporaries, and this meant that it would be constitutional and not absolute, and that it would not invade the liberties of the subject, which were guaranteed to him by the common law, with its underlying assumption, not that the ends of the state are paramount, but that the individual can do what he likes provided he keeps within the law.[1] Individualism in this sense is in accordance with the emphasis of Protestant Christianity, in which Locke shared, on the supreme importance of the individual soul; it is in accord, finally, with the philosophy unfolded in the *Essay concerning Human Understanding*, which is individualist in that it centres on the individual and the knowledge he acquires by the use of his own senses.

[1] Needless to say, the seventeenth-century constitution, though it had no universal suffrage, and in effect vested political supremacy in the hands of the landowning class, threatened individual liberty much less than the 'majority-rule democracy' of to-day.

III

GOVERNMENT BY CONSENT

'GOVERNMENT by consent' has for so long been a stock description of what is also loosely called parliamentary, or representative, or democratic, or popular government, that, as with many other pieces of current terminology, whatever sharpness of definition it may once have had has long since been worn off. Professor Plamenatz some years ago attempted to restore, or provide, a precise meaning for the phrase.[1] Strictly speaking, he argued, a government governs by consent only when its *right* to govern is conditional upon those governed having expressed the wish that it should govern them. It does not govern by consent simply because it in fact carries out the wishes of its subjects, or even when its policy is expressly framed to meet their wishes, or when the fulfilment of their wishes is a necessary condition for its ability to make its rule effective. Consent is essentially the granting of permission to someone to do something which he would not have a right to do without such permission; and government by consent, therefore, implies that the government's right to govern (not its power to do so, nor its actual policy) is created by the expression of the wishes of its subjects.

In the light of this test many governments which have been loosely called governments by consent are shown up as nothing of the kind. Queen Elizabeth I, for instance, is often said to have governed with the consent of her subjects, simply because she knew what they wanted her to do

[1] *Consent, Freedom and Political Obligation* (Oxford, 1938), esp. pp. 4 ff.

and acted accordingly; but in reality she was only a bene-volent and popular despot. Undoubtedly the idea of con-sent has sometimes been stretched a long way, and T. H. Green, indeed, went so far as to argue that no despot, however arbitrary, ever really governs simply by force alone, or against the general will.[1] The doctrine of the 'real will' is a further refinement of this kind of argument, by which all governments can be made out to be govern-ments by consent, so that even the worst tyrannies may be clothed with a specious respectability. Hitler used to pay lip-service to the virtues of peaceableness and good faith by pretending, when he invaded a country, that he was pro-tecting its inhabitants from some threat to their security. Similarly, even though these arguments do not convince us, they are interesting as evidence of the unwillingness of their ingenious authors wholly to abandon the old tradition of liberty, which the notion of consent enshrines.

They also imply the doctrine that the only rightful source of power is the will of the governed, even though that will may not find direct expression. This doctrine is widely current in modern times, especially in countries which have been influenced by the French Revolution; and even in England, though our parliamentary tradition is much older than that,[2] the frequently cited, if disputable, notion that a government can take no action unless speci-fically authorized to do so by a 'mandate' from the people implies the same doctrine that the people themselves are the only legitimate source of power.

[1] T. H. Green, *Principles of Political Obligation*, Lecture G. As against this, it must be admitted that he only counted Tsarist Russia as a state 'by a sort of courtesy' (ibid., § 132).

[2] The notion of the popular origins of political power is, of course, much older still. It is implied, for example, in the so-called *lex regia*, by which the emperors were supposed to exercise an *imperium* conveyed to them by the Roman people.

Locke took over the idea of consent, like most, if not all, of the tools in his workshop, from his predecessors and contemporaries in sixteenth- and seventeenth-century England, where it was already as well established, and as variously and loosely used, as it has been ever since. The idea of consent had descended to Locke's generation from the Middle Ages in which it had grown up, as a regular part of the doctrine of the functions of parliament, and I expect that it was often referred to, then as now, with little critical consideration of what it really meant. This is not the place to retrace its early history:[1] suffice it to say that it was closely connected with the idea of the sanctity of property, and developed largely as part of the mechanism by which medieval property-owners were induced to submit to taxation. It is not easy to say how far, in the Middle Ages, the consent regarded as necessary to the validity of taxation, or of other legislation as well, was thought of as the consent of individuals. At first unanimity was required;[2] but in course of time the notion of consent became involved, in its parliamentary setting, with the companion doctrine of representation, and, as both of these developed, their original meaning became obscured by much looseness of phraseology, if not of thought, and a considerable element of fiction. Consent no longer effectively safeguards the sanctity of private property if it ceases to be personal and individual; yet the practice grew up by which electors appointed representatives, or proxies, to give consent in their name, and once this step was taken, the individual element inevitably lost ground. It would soon be argued that the consent of a representative was

[1] See, e.g., M. V. Clarke, *Medieval Representation and Consent* (1936).

[2] In Henry III's reign Peter des Roches is said to have successfully claimed exemption from a tax to which he had not personally agreed (A. F. Pollard, *The Evolution of Parliament* (1920), p. 143).

as good as the consent of his constituents, and then that the representative chosen by a majority of constituents represented the whole body of constituents, and that the consent (in parliament) of a majority of representatives was binding on all the constituents, including those who had voted for unsuccessful candidates, and those whose representatives had voted the other way. I think that one reason why such far-reaching conclusions were possible was that they were propounded by lawyers accustomed to the use of legal fictions.[1] On the other hand, it would be a mistake to overstress the individual (and hence the fictitious) element in medieval thought on this subject. After all, if consent through representatives were only a convenient fiction, why should property-owners have let themselves be deceived by it? The consent required was not always a consent counted numerically, and so implying the doctrine of equality. A medieval monarch would sometimes quote the Latin tag that what touches all should be approved by all, but sometimes he would legislate after consulting only the magnates of his realm. Sometimes he would seek 'advice and consent', but his actions would be valid although he did not accept the advice tendered to him. Nor was it always a simple majority (*pars major*) which was counted, but sometimes the *pars potior et sanior*, or the *pars valentior*, which by no means necessarily implied a numerical majority.[2] Medieval lawyers equated the

[1] M. V. Clarke, op. cit., p. 286. Cf. C. H. McIlwain, *Constitutionalism Ancient and Modern* (Ithaca, N.Y., 1940), pp. 116, 117.

[2] Sir Robert Filmer noticed this point, in *Patriarcha* and *Observations concerning the Originall of Government* (1652): *Works* (Blackwell, ed. Laslett, 1949), pp. 82, 243–4, 255. He concluded that this sort of argument in defence of popular rights made no sense, and he preferred therefore to base the authority of government on divine right. The Commons, he pointed out, were summoned *ad faciendum et consentiendum*, to perform and consent to what was ordained by king and council. This did not imply a power to dissent, so that they had no real choice at all (ibid., p. 135).

action of a representative with the action of his constituents because the constituency was regarded as a community rather than as a collection of individuals, and the notion of consent was connected with an idea of organic continuity, binding not only contemporaries but successive generations together in membership of the same society. Thus Hooker, in a well-known passage, argued that 'to be commanded we do consent, when that society whereof we are part hath at any time before consented. . . . Wherefore as any man's deed past is good as long as himself continueth; so the act of a public society of men done five hundred years sithence standeth as theirs who presently are the same societies, because corporations are immortal; we were then alive in our predecessors, and they in their successors do live still.'[1]

Is this a thought more profound than crude individualism is capable of? Or is it just a muddled thought, involving a fiction in a transcendental disguise? An answer to this would involve finding an answer to a kindred question, which has received similarly diverse interpretations—the question whether societies and corporations are 'real persons', or whether corporate personality is fictitious, and the only real persons are individual human beings. I shall not add to the already considerable volume of discussion on this subject, except to suggest that here, as in other matters where apparently contradictory views are put forward, each expresses one side of the truth, but falsifies the truth as a whole, when it emphasizes its own side to the exclusion of the other. It is a commonplace to say that a group, or a community, is something different from and more than what its individual members are con-

[1] T. Hooker, *Eccl. Pol.* I. x. 8. Locke quoted the sentences preceding and following this passage in a note to *Second Treatise*, § 134; it is perhaps significant that he omitted this passage itself.

sidered separately and apart from their membership of it; it is different, too, from what they are considered as an aggregate. The difficulty, however, is to say precisely in what this difference consists. I have no neat formula to offer to epitomize the nature of the relationship between the individual and the community. Neat formulae, indeed, should be mistrusted, for they are apt to rest on analogies, and therefore to be misleading, because they contain only part of the truth. Some thinkers have said that the individual stands to the community like a part to the whole, or like a limb or member to an organism; others have seen in this relationship an embodiment of the 'concrete universal'. None of these analogies is entirely satisfactory, though each may illustrate one aspect of the truth. The whole truth of this relationship is *sui generis* and unique: or rather it is manifold, for its content will vary according to the character of the community in question. We may come to understand it by analysis and careful description, but I doubt if it can be defined in terms of something else. We shall hesitate, therefore, to believe that there is a super-personality of the community over and above the personalities of its members. Yet without some sense of corporate solidarity a community could hardly maintain its existence, and the narrow selfishness of crude individualism is as inadequate an explanation of human conduct as were the motives of the 'economic man' of the classical economists. In the case of a political community this sense of solidarity will be built up by its history and traditions, its manners and customs, and by habituation in a life guided and moulded by its permanent institutions. It is this sense which makes a nation acknowledge and support—'consent to'—the government which has come to be established in the course of its history, even though individuals may dislike and oppose the administration actually in power, and may indeed have voted against it at a general election.

Can we say that a parliamentary democratic government is a government by consent, whereas a totalitarian dictatorship is not, because under a democratic government there is an opposition which can vote? In what sense does an outvoted opposition consent to the legislation of the government in power? Can conservatives, for example, rightly be said to consent to the nationalization of industries by a socialist government? Is this not to stretch the meaning of consent too far, and ought we not rather to say that they acquiesce perhaps, but only very unwillingly? But then, why after all do they finally acquiesce? Is it not because they are not prepared to press their opposition to extremes, which in the end would mean revolution or civil war? And is not the ultimate reason why parliamentary government and opposition have broken down in so many countries, that the opposing sides are too deeply divided for such acquiescence to be possible? For parliamentary government to work, the minority at any time must have a reasonable prospect of winning support for its point of view and, sooner or later, becoming the majority. There must, therefore, be a sizeable uncommitted 'floating' vote, so that the opposition is potentially an alternative government. But where majority and minority are fixed and permanent sections of a community, so deeply divided by religion, or ideology, or nationality, or race, or colour, that the section in power uses its advantage to oppress or impose its will on the rest, such acquiescence can hardly be relied on, and in such circumstances a parliamentary constitution is likely to prove unworkable. Where conditions are favourable to the working of a parliamentary system, and an outvoted opposition is willing, for the time being to accept government by its opponents, it means, in

effect, that both sides agree to abide by—'consent to'—
the rules of the game, or, in other words, the constitution
itself.[1] In this sense we may say that a party which finds
itself in opposition consents even to the legislation of its
opponents, because loyalty to the constitution involves its
accepting the consequences of the verdict of the electorate.[2]
This does not mean that we need accept all the implications of the doctrine of the general will, or the theory that
the people are the only source of legitimate power and that
the authority of government is therefore derived from a
popular mandate. The doctrine of consent has sometimes
been taken to mean this, but it is certainly not what the
doctrine meant in its early days. When a king governed or
legislated with the consent of the barons, or of parliament,
the authority was his; it was not granted to him by them.
In the past this probably involved some element of divine
right, a doctrine which would find little acceptance today;
but, if we have abandoned that, its place is not necessarily
taken by the doctrine of popular sovereignty (which may
come in practice to mean something like the divine right
of majorities), and it can be argued that the function of the
electorate and of parliament is still to give consent (or else
to criticize and refuse consent) to the authority of government, but not to create it.[3]

Mr. Plamenatz made consent a question of the *right* of

[1] In fact it is only when parties can treat politics as a game and not as
a war that parliamentary government is possible. This means that they
must agree about fundamentals, and differ only about less radical matters.
Their refusal or inability to do so is one of the excuses for dictatorships.

[2] Rousseau, it will be remembered, declared that 'the citizen gives his
consent to all the laws, including those which are passed in spite of his
opposition, and even those which punish him when he dares to break any
of them' (*Contrat Social*, iv. 1). I am not certain exactly what he meant by this
paradox, but I take it to be not so much a consequence of the acceptance of
a historic constitution as a corollary of his doctrine of the general will.

[3] Cf. L. S. Amery, *Thoughts on the Constitution* (Oxford, 1947), p. 15.

a government to govern. If we ask what makes our government the legitimate government of our country, and by what right it governs, surely the answer must be that it is because it is the government which has obtained power in accordance with the constitution.[1] Its right, in fact, is an historic right—a prescriptive right if you like—rooted in the effective exercise of power by successive governments for ages. This is why it receives the loyal, if sometimes grudging, consent even of its most convinced opponents; whereas an alien government, however benevolent, which attempted to impose its rule from outside by conquest would meet with resistance as well as resentment, and such resistance would be commended as patriotic.[2]

The notion of consent has had such a long history that it has inevitably come in time to acquire differences of meaning. It began with the literal meaning of personal consent (to taxation, for example), but this is no reason for liberals and individualists later on to assert the principle that the personal consent of the governed is the only legitimate basis of government. This proves an impossible theory of society, but the ingenious doctrines of the idealists were in effect an attempt to preserve the principle at the price of so stretching the meaning of consent as to obliterate its difference from coercion by despotism. Such abuses of the word called for a protest in the name of accuracy and precision, if not of common sense. The conclusion Mr. Plamenatz came to is that consent, strictly defined, is only

[1] I do not mean that the constitution is above the government, as in the U.S.A. In England, of course, the government (with the consent of parliament) can alter the constitution, and that is one way in which the constitution has been modified in course of time and brought up to date.

[2] Some people will resist any government, however legitimate, and break the law as far as they dare or can; but though any existing government will treat the breach of its laws as a crime, there is a valid distinction between criminal and patriotic or moral resistance.

one among a number of possible foundations for political obligation. Where it is present it constitutes an additional obligation to obedience, but a government may, and many governments lawfully do, claim obedience from people whose consent has never been asked or given. This is certainly true if consent is to be kept to Mr. Plamenatz's strict definition; but I doubt if in practice it has ever been used quite so precisely as this, and though it is a salutary task of philosophy to refine common speech, and reveal the implications of the language we sometimes thoughtlessly use, the fact remains that in the course of its long history the phrase, being not a technical term but a term of common speech, has had a number of meanings, and I doubt if we are entitled to say that only one of these is correct, and to dismiss all the rest as examples of loose thinking.

What Locke and his Whig contemporaries were chiefly concerned to do was to refute the claim of absolute monarchs to arbitrary power. In the seventeenth century prescription did not seem secure enough a foundation for the right of a legitimate government to govern: in the face of disputed successions something more certain was needed. Hence, among other reasons, the ready acceptance of the doctrine of the divine right of kings: hence, too, in opposition, the doctrine of the equally divine, or at any rate natural, imprescriptible rights of man, and its corollary that no man can be deprived of his natural condition of freedom and equality and 'subjected to the political power of another, without his own consent'.[1] It is sometimes thought that this individualist position was Locke's characteristic contribution to political theory; or at any rate that, if it did not originate with him, he made it the basis of his solution of the problem of political obligation, so that it came to be specially associated with

[1] *Second Treatise*, § 95.

him.[1] Moreover, he had to strain the principle of individual consent to breaking-point in order to make it
fit the facts of experience, notably in his theory that every
resident in a country could be presumed to have given tacit
consent to its government. We shall return to this later, but
it is easy enough to point out that if consent means no more
than this, it is no safeguard whatever against the exercise
of tyranny. Many critics, therefore, especially those un-
sympathetic to Locke's general political attitude, simply
discredit him as a thinker, and treat the dubious subter-
fuges (tacit consent, &c.) and inconsistencies into which
he was driven as so many nails in the coffin of individualism. With it they would gladly bury natural rights, the
social contract, and the whole liberal apparatus, leaving
the way clear for the idealist doctrine of the absorption
of the individual in the social whole under the majestic
authority of the state.

It is questionable, however, whether this account of
Locke's political theory is not a serious distortion both of
his aims and of his achievements. Of his aims, because it
appears to assume that he set out to construct from first
principles an abstract doctrine of political obligation; of
his achievements, because there are numerous other passages in his *Treatises of Government* which suggest a different
interpretation of the place of consent in his theory of
government from the one outlined above. Admittedly,
there are a good many places—some twenty in fact—in
the *Second Treatise* which lend colour to an extreme individualist interpretation of his position. In the first place,
his use of the qualifying epithet, 'own', or, where more
than one man is being spoken of, the plural *consents*, would

[1] Cf. C. E. Vaughan's chapter on Locke in *Studies in the History of Political Philosophy before and after Rousseau* (Manchester, 1925), i. 130 ff., and see p. 27 above.

seem to mean that the consent is to be individual and personal, and to exclude vicarious or merely collective consent.[1] Thus he affirms that 'all men are naturally in that state (sc. the state of nature), and remain so, till by their own consents they make themselves members of some politic society'.[2] In his chapter 'Of the beginning of political societies' this individualism is stated even more emphatically: no man, he writes, 'can be subjected to the political power of another, without his own consent';[3] a civil society, therefore, can only be made by each member 'agreeing with other men to join and unite into a community', and in the next paragraph he tells us that to 'make' a community in this way involves 'the consent of every individual'.[4] The chapter concludes with an equally uncompromising declaration that nothing can make any man a subject or a member of a commonwealth 'but his actually entering into it by positive engagement and express promise and compact. This is . . . that consent which makes any one a member of any commonwealth.'[5] Promises extorted by force, moreover, do not constitute consent,[6] and although a conqueror may have reduced the fathers to subjection, he has no lawful authority over the children 'but by their own consent, whatever he may drive them to say or do'.[7] The same insistence on the necessity for personal consent is a marked feature of Locke's theory of property. 'The supreme power cannot take from any man any part of his property without his own consent':[8]

[1] Cf. also the passages quoted from the early treatise on the power of the civil magistrate, below, pp. 202, 203.

[2] *Second Treatise*, § 15.

[3] § 95.

[4] § 96; cf. § 106: 'The beginning of politic society depends upon the consent of the individuals to join into and make one society.'

[5] § 122.   [6] § 186.
[7] § 189.   [8] § 138; cf. 139.

in fact, the nature of property is such that 'without a man's consent it cannot be taken from him'.[1]

In its extreme form the doctrine of consent might mean that a man is bound only by what he now consents to; for if we deny this, while holding that individual consent is the only rightful source of power, we raise the question why even a single objector should be coerced, possibly against his own conscience. But this is obviously a completely anarchical principle,[2] and it conflicts also with the commonly accepted idea that it is generally a moral duty to keep one's promises. Hence the doctrine of consent has usually been held in the modified form in which a man is bound in future by what he once consented to, even though he has since changed his mind. In other words, consent does not mean only present consent, but includes past commitments. Now Locke did not advocate anarchy. His object rather was to explain how men could have emerged from the state of nature and become associated in legitimate political societies, in which they could rightly be required to obey the government. He therefore does not maintain the extreme individualist position. He affirms the moral duty of keeping promises, for he bases it on natural, not positive, law,[3] and he makes it clear that consent once given is irrevocable: unless the government is dissolved or publicly cuts a man off from membership of the community, 'he that has once by actual agreement and any express declaration given his consent to be of any commonweal is perpetually and indispensably obliged to

[1] *Second Treatise*, § 193.

[2] But this was really the attitude of the people alluded to at the beginning of J. S. Mill's *Liberty*, who were disappointed because self-government turned out to be 'not the government of each by himself, but of each by all the rest', or even by a bare majority of the rest.

[3] 'Truth and keeping of faith belong to men as men, and not as members of society' (§ 14).

be and remain unalterably a subject to it, and can never be again in the liberty of the state of nature'.[1]

Now, if this is all that consent means, it could include the total alienation to a Hobbesian sovereign, once for all in the past, of his subjects' liberties. But the resulting arbitrary power would be precisely the kind of government we commonly do *not* mean when we speak of government by consent. Locke certainly did not write in order to advocate a Hobbesian despotism, nor, on the other hand, did he advocate anarchy, or the continuance of the state of nature. His objective was constitutional government; but what keeps such a government constitutional, or prevents it from becoming arbitrary, is not, in Locke, any effectively continuing personal consent, by which the wishes of individual subjects can act on it as a brake or check. The government is controlled by being subject still to the law of nature. It has a duty to fulfil its trust, which means to govern for the 'public good', by settled, known laws and not by arbitrary decrees, and it knows that the threat of revolution lies in the background in case it seriously fails to do so. The element of consent figures prominently in Locke in the formal inauguration of the state, but in the actual operation of government it is relegated to a back seat, and even that it only retains in a shape so modified and reduced as to destroy its original significance.

Though every individual's consent was necessary at the inauguration of a political community, this does not imply that political liberty is the same as the liberty of the state of nature: 'or else this original compact . . . would signify nothing, and be no compact. . . . For what appearance would there be of any compact? What new engagement if he were no farther tied by any decrees of the society,

[1] § 121.

than he himself thought fit and *did actually consent to*?'[1]
This is Locke's first important exception to the principle
of individual consent, and it leads immediately to another,
namely, that the consent of the majority must 'in reason
be received as the act of the whole and conclude every
individual'. Otherwise, considering the various reasons of
health and business which would prevent many from
attending the public assembly, and the 'variety of opinions
and contrariety of interests' unavoidably found in all
'collections of men', society would hardly outlast the day
of its birth, if 'nothing but the consent of every individual
can make anything to be the act of the whole.' Joining a
society upon such terms would be 'only like Cato's coming
into the theatre, only to go out again'.[2] Individual consent,
therefore, is required only at the initiation of a political
community: once the community has been made, it is
made 'one body, with a power to act as one body, which
is only by the will and determination of the majority'.[3]
Locke's justification for this is practical—that the community cannot otherwise continue to exist and act in
unity: his explanation of it, however, is mechanical. What
'acts' (i.e. moves) a community is nothing but the consent
of its individual members, so that if it is to continue as one
body and not break up again, it must 'move one way'; and
the way it will move will be 'that whither the greater force
carries it, which is the consent of the majority'. When
individuals, by consent, joined the community, they agreed
it should continue as one body; 'and so every one is bound
by that consent to be concluded by the majority'.

At first sight this explanation of the majority-principle
may seem to be an improvement on the rather unreal and
artificial theory, to be found in numerous foreign writers
(e.g. Pufendorf), that majority-decisions are binding

---

[1] *Second Treatise*, § 97 (my italics).   [2] § 98.   [3] § 96.

because one of the express terms of the original compact was that they should be so. In effect, however, Locke's theory comes to much the same thing, for he tells us that when men agree 'to make one body politic' this implies acceptance of an obligation to submit to majority-decisions.[1] At the same time he bases the right of the majority on 'the law of nature and reason',[2] but he makes no attempt to show why the law of nature and reason gives the majority this right, beyond the further assertion that 'where the majority cannot conclude the rest, there they cannot act as one body, and consequently will be immediately dissolved again'.[3] As Mr. Willmoore Kendall has pointed out, Locke greatly exaggerates in maintaining that unless majority-rule is accepted the only alternative to unanimity is the disintegration of the community, and a few pages on he writes of people consenting to the rule of a single person, such as the head of a family.[4] And even if majority-rule were the only practicable alternative to unanimity, this would not in itself constitute a natural right in majorities to make decisions.[5] Locke's argument, therefore, that majority-rule is based on the law of nature is not impressive; on the contrary, the rules governing majority-votes are often in practice quite definitely artificial, and Locke himself allows for cases where the members uniting to form a community may have 'expressly agreed in any number greater than the majority'.[6] The truth is that the whole principle that the decision of a majority is binding on all (and whether it be a two-thirds majority or a bare majority makes no difference in principle) is quite artificial: convenient, no doubt, but by no means natural or

[1] § 97.   [2] § 96.   [3] § 98.   [4] § 112.
[5] Willmoore Kendall, 'John Locke and the Doctrine of Majority-Rule' (*Illinois Studies in the Social Sciences*, xxvi, no. 2, 1941), p. 114.
[6] *Second Treatise*, § 99.

inevitable. As far as nature goes, if it goes anywhere, the only binding decision is a unanimous one, where a minority—where even a single objector—has a *liberum veto*, as in the Polish diet. Burke pointed out that the majority-principle was 'one of the most violent fictions of positive law', to which men could only be brought to submit 'by long habits of obedience, by a sort of discipline in society'.[1] He denied, accordingly, the right of a majority of the French people to change their government by revolution, and if the English or any other people claimed the same right, he replied that they had 'just the same undoubtedly. That is, none at all.'[2] This is going rather far, for though a majority has no natural right to conclude a minority, decision by majority-vote may have a stronger argument in its favour than mere convenience. Consent, Mr. Willmoore Kendall has suggested, is additive,[3] and it may be argued that a decision on which all have been consulted, and which is supported by a large number, is preferable to, and more binding than, one on which nobody has been consulted and which is supported only by a few. Locke knew, and in effect was saying, that in societies recalcitrants have to be coerced, so that when a man consents to join a commonwealth he consents to accept decisions he may not approve of himself, and rightly so, because this is implicit in the nature of life in a community. The question is, though, whether the right of the community to coerce recalcitrants flows from mere numerical superiority or from some more esoteric characteristic of community life. Locke did not consider this question, but he was evidently aware that there was a question to be solved. I think the main reason why he was

[1] 'Appeal from the New to the Old Whigs', in *Works*, vi. 211.
[2] Ibid., p. 201.
[3] Willmoore Kendall, op. cit., p. 117.

satisfied with a mechanical explanation was that majority-decision had so long been established in English parliamentary practice that it seemed 'natural' and could be taken for granted.

That this was so is suggested, I think, by the way the notion of consent was used among the Levellers at the close of the Civil War, albeit in association with a radical egalitarianism and a demand for manhood, or at any rate a greatly extended, suffrage and equal electoral districts, as proposed in the *Agreement of the People*. A typical example is in Col. Rainborough's well-known remarks in the debates of the Council of the Army at Putney in October 1647. It was because 'the poorest he that is in England hath a life to live, as the greatest he', that Rainborough thought 'it's clear, that every man that is to live under a government ought first by his own consent to put himself under that government'.[1] Like some of the passages we have noticed in Locke, this seems to be a plea for an extreme individualism, but in the next sentence it appears that a man's right to give 'his own consent' to a government is satisfied by allowing him 'a voice to put himself under it'. This indeed brings consent within the bounds of practical possibility, but at the cost of reducing it to a mere right to be consulted; and Rainborough seems completely oblivious (he even thinks that he is using consent 'in a strict sense') of the fact that, on the basis of individualism, the claim of a majority to command obedience is a problem calling for explanation. Locke was aware of this problem, but in practice his answer was even less individualist than Rainborough's. Rainborough at any rate demanded a vote for all, but Locke, though he would have welcomed a redistribution of seats and the disfranchisement of decayed boroughs, tacitly assumed the

[1] A. S. P. Woodhouse, *Puritanism and Liberty* (1938), p. 53.

continuation of the narrow traditional electoral system which restricted the vote to a small class of property-owners.

We may now consider a further departure from the principle of individual consent. It is a man's express consent which makes him a member of a society, but he may also be bound as a subject, and 'be looked on to have consented', without having expressed his consent at all. A man gives 'tacit consent' if he 'hath any possession or enjoyment of any part of the dominions of any government', and is obliged to obey its laws 'whether this his possession be of land to him or his heirs for ever, or a lodging only for a week; or whether it be barely travelling freely on the highway': tacit consent to a government may indeed be presumed from merely being within its territories.[1] Now genuine consent may certainly be given tacitly as well as expressly: there may, for example, be cases where a man's consent to something may properly be presumed from his not expressing a refusal. But it is easy to show (e.g. from the existence of conspirators and criminals) that merely travelling in a country does not imply a willingness to obey its laws.[2] It may indeed be held that a traveller is obliged to obey the laws of a country he travels in, but this is not to say that he is so obliged because he has consented.[3] It is so obviously absurd to presume that Guy Fawkes's presence in the cellars of the Palace of Westminster implied his tacit consent to the laws against the Roman Catholics that one is driven to consider whether Locke can have meant anything of the kind. He knew well enough of the existence of plotters and lawbreakers, and was indeed seek-

[1] *Second Treatise*, § 119.

[2] Cf. J. P. Plamenatz, op. cit., p. 7.

[3] It may be noticed that in § 73 Locke does not mention consent, but simply remarks that there is 'always annexed to the enjoyment of land a submission to the government of the country of which that land is a part'.

ing a justification for the right of governments to punish
them. His argument is so ill thought out that it is hard to
know what to make of it, but it seems clear that he recognized that a basic necessity for the continued existence of
a state is the obligation of everyone to obey the laws.
Having previously said that nobody who has not consented is so obliged, he had to assume that people who
have not explicitly consented have done so tacitly. But if
consent can be so watered down as to be implied by mere
presence in a country, it is no safeguard whatever against
tyranny. It should be observed, however, that Locke did
not argue that 'submitting to the laws of any country,
living quietly and enjoying privileges and protection under
them' make a man a member of a society. He distinguished
this 'local protection and homage', which lasts only as
long as a man remains within the territories of a government, and can be broken off at any time if a man prefers
to go and live elsewhere (either joining another commonwealth or agreeing with others to found a new one *in vacuis
locis*), from full membership of a commonwealth, which is
perpetual. Tacit consent, it appears, binds only to the
obedience due from resident aliens, whereas full membership involves 'actually entering into it by positive engagement, and express promise and compact'.[1]

This is all very well for the original incorporating
members (assuming that Locke meant his account of the
formation of states by agreement to be taken as literally
and historically true, which is doubtful), but how about
later generations? Have they consented, and expressly too?
Yes, Locke replies. A father cannot 'oblige his posterity to
that government of which he himself was a subject': they
may 'choose what society they will join themselves to',
though 'if they will enjoy the inheritance of their ancestors,

[1] § 122.

they must take it on the same terms their ancestors had it'.[1] This gives fathers an advantage over their children, by which they commonly keep them in obedience even when they are past minority, and often subject them to some particular political power. Paternal power naturally lasts no longer than the minority of the children, and though in the first ages of the world 'family governments readily sprang up under paternal authority' (often nothing more was required to establish a monarchical power than to permit 'the father to exercise alone in his family that executive power of the law of nature which every free man naturally hath'), nevertheless, where grown-up children submitted to this, it was only by their 'express or tacit consent'.[2] Consent here seems to be a synonym for acquiescence, and Locke later admits that if we look back into history we shall generally find that governments are monarchical in form and took their origin from paternal power.[3] But he insists that men are not bound to submit to their fathers' authority, nor can a father by any compact of his own bind his children or posterity. In effect a son cannot enjoy his father's possessions except by joining the society and accepting the same conditions, but Locke maintains that in so doing he voluntarily submits to its government, and it is none the less consent, although 'being given separately in their turns, as each comes to be of age, and not in a multitude together, people take no notice of it'.[4] Locke defends this argument by reference to

[1] *Second Treatise*, § 73; cf. § 191.

[2] § 74. In the next section the children's consent is called 'tacit and scarce avoidable' ('tacit and almost natural' in early editions).

[3] § 105 ff. In § 110 he gives an unobjectionable picture of a family growing by degrees into a commonwealth, with the father's authority passing to his eldest son; 'every one in his turn growing up under it tacitly submitted to it; and the easiness and equality of it not offending any one, every one acquiesced, till time seemed to have confirmed it, and settled a right of succession by prescription'.   [4] § 117.

the practice of the French and English governments in cases like that of a child born in France to English parents. Such a child does not automatically become an English subject, but has to ask leave to be admitted as one: nor can the King of France claim him, for his father can remove him from France and bring him up as he likes. The child born abroad is, in fact, stateless, and so, Locke argues, it is plain 'by the practice of governments themselves, as well as by the law of right reason, that a child is born a subject of no country or government'. Until he comes of age he is 'under his father's tuition and authority', and then he can decide for himself what state he will join.[1] Since Locke's time the laws of nationality have been hardened in all countries, and the position he described no longer holds today; but this does not necessarily invalidate for his own age an argument which he seems to have based on his own observation, correct or incorrect, of the practice of governments then prevailing.

It is more than questionable, however, whether the fact that the law treated the age of twenty-one as the age when a child became adult really supports the notion Locke seems to have that every child, on reaching that age, voluntarily adopts adult citizenship and so 'consents' to obey the government established in his country.[2] In his chapter 'Of Conquest'[3] Locke presses the notion of personal consent to a length which can never have been recognized in practice by any government. He argues, not only that an aggressor in an unjust war acquires no rights over a people he conquers, so that they are entitled to

[1] § 118.
[2] We should remember, however, that oaths of allegiance and similar personal declarations played a more prominent part in the seventeenth century than they do today. See J. Dunn, *The Political Thought of John Locke* (Cambridge, 1969), pp. 135 ff.
[3] Chap. xvi.

revolt against him, but that a conqueror even in a just war acquires only strictly limited rights. In the first place, 'he gets no power by his conquest over his own people who fought on his side'.[1] Of the people conquered, he gets power only 'over those who have actually assisted, concurred or consented to that unjust force that is used against him'.[2] He cannot touch 'the lives or fortunes of those who engaged not in the war, nor . . . the possessions even of those who were actually engaged in it'.[3] These must be reserved for their innocent wives and children.[4] Locke admits that conquerors seldom trouble themselves with such refinements, but 'willingly permit the confusion of war to sweep all together', and that his doctrine will seem strange, 'it being so quite contrary to the practice of the world'. It might, indeed, place an intolerable strain on the unity of a belligerent nation. But it is a striking testimony to the seriousness of Locke's belief in the principle of consent.

It would seem, then, that Locke's theory begins with the principle that a man need only obey a government to whose authority he has given his personal consent. This principle is incompatible with the effective exercise of coercive authority by government, but rather than abandon it Locke qualifies it by the doctrine that after originally

[1] Thus the title of the English monarchy cannot be founded on the Norman conquest, for even if William had had a right to invade this island, the dominion he acquired 'could reach no further than to the Saxons and Britons that were then inhabitants of this country. The Normans that came with him, and helped to conquer, and all descended from them, are free men, and not subjects by conquest' (§ 177). This is Locke's passing allusion to the controversy between Tory historians such as Robert Brady and Whigs such as William Petyt and James Tyrrell, who fervently asserted the immemorial antiquity of the English constitution, and denied that the Norman conquest had been a conquest at all. On this see J. G. A. Pocock, *The Ancient Constitution and the Feudal Law* (Cambridge, 1957); Q. Skinner, 'History and Ideology in the English Revolution', in *Historical Journal*, viii (1965), pp. 151–78.   [2] § 179.   [3] § 178.   [4] §§ 182, 183.

consenting to become a citizen a man is bound by the decision of the majority. Furthermore, his consent need not be explicit, but can be given tacitly in various ways. So far, Locke seems to mean by consent personal consent, even though it may be modified and qualified. Besides these qualifications, however, there are a number of passages where Locke used the term 'consent' more loosely and vaguely, and we cannot be certain whether he always meant by it the personal consent of individuals. A phrase he often used, for example, is 'the consent of the people';[1] or he may simply remark that 'the liberty of man in society is to be under no other legislative power but that established by consent in the commonwealth',[2] without specifying whether this consent is to be taken in a strictly personal sense.[3] He appears not to notice any difference between strict individual consent and the vague consent of 'the people', or, for that matter, of the majority. He tells us, for example, that a law is only binding if it has 'its sanction from that legislative which the public has chosen and appointed'. Without this it would lack what 'is absolutely necessary to its being a law, the consent of the society'; and then in the next breath that no government can have a power to make laws over a society 'but by their own consent, and by authority received from them'.[4] Then again

[1] e.g. §§ 104, 112, 142, 168, 175, 198, 212, 216, 227.   [2] § 22.

[3] Cf. also the unspecified use of the word 'consent' in §§ 38, 50, 81, 102, 103, 105, 179.

[4] § 134. In a footnote he quotes Hooker, to the effect that the power of making laws to command 'whole politic societies of men' belongs properly 'unto the same entire societies', so that it is mere tyranny if princes make laws except either by immediate and personal commission from God, or else 'by authority derived at first from their consent, upon whose persons they impose laws'. He also quotes Hooker's remark that 'to be commanded we do consent when that society, whereof we be a part, hath at any time before consented, without revoking the same after by the like universal agreement'; but he omits the intervening passage where Hooker stresses more clearly the solidarity of a continuing society (above, p. 56, n. 1).

there are passages where Locke simply identified action by a man's representative with action by himself, as, for example, where the commonwealth is entitled to employ a man's force for the execution of its judgements 'which, indeed, are his own judgements, they being made by himself or his representative'.[1] A still more striking passage is his reconciliation of taxation with the sanctity of private property, where he declares that everyone enjoying the protection provided by government must pay his share of the expense of maintaining it; 'but still it must be with his own consent, i.e. the consent of the majority giving it either by themselves or their representatives chosen by them'.[2] Can Locke, we may ask ourselves in astonishment, really have thought that the consent of a majority of representatives was the same as a man's own consent, from which it is, in fact, twice removed? It is easy to conclude from this and similar passages that Locke was a loose thinker and that his arguments need not be taken seriously. I think this is a grave misinterpretation of Locke's real aim. He appears to state his political theory in general philosophical terms, as if it were a purely logical deduction from general principles, but if we read between the lines we recognize the historic features of the English seventeenth-century constitution. As Mr. Dunn has remarked, his purpose was not to propound a general theory of how governments should be organized, and the idea that all political decisions should be put to a popular vote would have seemed to him, as indeed it would to everybody in the seventeenth century except the Levellers, both dangerous and absurd.[3] In form, Locke derived political

[1] *Second Treatise*, § 88.

[2] § 140. Cf. § 141, where the legislative 'must not raise taxes on the property of the people without the consent of the people, given by themselves or their deputies'.

[3] See J. Dunn, 'Consent in the Political Theory of John Locke', in

power 'from its original', in order that men might 'understand it aright',[1] but 'aright' really meant in the light of the philosophy of the Whigs rather than that of Filmer and the Tories. It is true that he claimed to make good the king's title 'in the consent of the people', but we shall undervalue his success in this if we dismiss his efforts because it turns out that the consent of the people is not the same as the continual and personal consent of every individual. T. H. Green remarked that 'the doctrine that the rights of government are founded on the consent of the governed is a confused way of stating the truth that the institutions by which man . . . comes to do what he sees that he must, as distinct from what he would like, express a conception of a common good'.[2] At bottom, I think, something like this was really Locke's position, even though he failed to state it clearly, and continued to write in a loose way in terms of consent. Locke appears to start from a theoretical mass of right-possessing individuals in a state of nature, but when he comes to discuss the operation of government he thinks in terms of his own countrymen under the English constitution of his own day. The state of nature and its whole concomitant apparatus of natural rights and the social contract was the regular stock-in-trade of the political writers of his age. He adopted all this because he could hardly help doing so, and because it was what the readers of political treatises expected and accepted. But what he was really doing, under the guise of erecting a form of government on the basis of freely consenting individuals, was to describe the operation of the traditional English constitution, and interpret it in terms of the Whig political philosophy current in his

---

Historical Journal, x (1967), p. 154, and his *The Political Thought of John Locke* (Cambridge, 1969), p. 128.

[1] § 4.   [2] *Principles of Political Obligation*, § 116.

age.[1] The notion of consent, never strictly analysed, and involving some element of legal fiction, had come to be embodied in this constitution in the course of its historical development, and was already so well established (particularly with respect to taxation and legislation) by the time Locke inherited it that he (and no doubt his readers also) found no need to subject it to a close analysis and scrutiny. Under such a scrutiny, I think we must conclude, the notion may seem self-contradictory, and it might therefore be wiser for us to abandon it. Yet it is so deeply embedded in our history and our habitual ways of speech and thought that perhaps this is scarcely possible.

If we retain the phrase, we should be careful to dissociate it from an indefensible individualism, just as on the other hand we need not read into it all the ingenuities of the idealist school. Its historic role has been as the mark of a régime which is willingly accepted and supported by its subjects because it is constitutional, representative, and parliamentary; which preserves the rights of man (and this, we need not fear to add, means the rights of individual men); which respects the consciences of individuals and the views of minorities, and allows political opposition (notwithstanding that when laws have been passed it enforces them): as distinct from a régime which treats individuals as mere means to the achievement of power as an end in itself, which tolerates no opposition, or even difference of opinion, and enforces its will by means of concentration camps and a secret police. This is a broad distinction between types of government which is easily recognizable today, and which is not invalidated by the existence of borderline cases, whether they be outwardly mild dictatorships, like Dr. Salazar's régime in Portugal,

[1] Cf. E. S. de Beer, 'Locke and English Liberalism', in J. W. Yolton (ed.), *John Locke: Problems and Perspectives* (Cambridge, 1969), pp. 34–44.

or apparently democratic governments which unfairly weight the scales in favour of one of the parties, as has been the practice of the government of Northern Ireland.

'Government by consent' may remain, therefore, as an historic and serviceable, if loose, description of a constitutional type of government, not because individuals ever personally agreed to accept it, but because it is sensitive to public opinion, with which it is kept in touch by representative institutions and a free press, and does not have to stifle opposition by force.[1] England's contribution to the history of the world has been pre-eminently the development of a workable government of this type—it has been many other things as well, but pre-eminently this—and its government is workable largely because it has been the product of a historical process of growth and development. The great contribution of Locke, and of his Whig contemporaries who accepted his views, was that by his analysis of this constitution at a crucial period of its growth, and by making its operation appear to be in accord with rational principles, he signally helped it to develop further on constitutional lines, instead of being diverted from them and becoming assimilated to the absolutist monarchies then prevalent abroad.

[1] In this modified, non-individualist sense the consent which supports and maintains a government *is* present consent, and this is the only kind of consent which can support a government. The distinction between present consent and past commitments (cf. p. 64 above) is irrelevant in this sense, and only arises when consent is interpreted individually.

IV

LOCKE'S THEORY OF PROPERTY

LOCKE's theory of property is one of the most prominent and distinctive features of his system of politics. In recent years its interpretation has given rise to controversy, but to critics of an earlier generation it seemed to mark him out as essentially and primarily an individualist. Not content, as many contractarians were, with a political theory which made men exchange their natural liberty for security and protection, Locke, it was often pointed out, was careful to insist that private property was an institution which, so far from owing its existence to civil society, had existed in the state of nature itself, and the prime task of government was to preserve it unharmed. 'The reason why men enter into society is the preservation of their property.'[1] It was generally assumed, by Locke as well as other contemporary writers of the school of natural law, that in the earliest times everything was common, by which was meant, not that there was any positive communism or common ownership of property, but simply that nothing belonged to anyone in particular (just as nobody today owns the air or the sea), and men just helped themselves to what they needed from nature's free supply.[2] At this point Locke's theory diverged from the usual view, according to which appropriation—helping oneself—did not create genuine, i.e. legally recog-

[1] *Second Treatise*, § 222.
[2] Cf., e.g., Pufendorf, *De Jure Naturae et Gentium*, IV. iv. 4; Grotius, *De Jure Belli et Pacis*, II. ii. 2.

nized, property. This could only be the product of contract
or agreement, and so could only come into existence with
the state itself. It might be created by a branch of the
social contract, men agreeing, when they entered into
society, that what anyone had appropriated for his own
use should be recognized as belonging to him, and should
be protected by law against interference by others. Some
writers believed that the institution of property was the
subject of a separate contract, apart from and subsequent
to the actual inauguration of the state.[1] Differences on
such points, however, were of relatively minor importance
in comparison with the general principle that property
was contractual, and that it did not precede but followed,
or at most accompanied, the creation of the state. Hence
it could be, and often was, argued that property could only
be held on such conditions as the state thought fit to
impose, and that governments had overriding powers to
levy contributions from citizens, by taxation or requisition,
for defence and other public purposes.

In Locke, however, there was not only possession but
ownership in the state of nature, and men came together
to form civil society with natural rights, and the right of
property first among them, already in their hands. The
state did not create property, but was itself created in order
to protect it. No government, therefore, can take 'the
whole or any part of the subjects' property without their
own consent',[2] and though it is fitting that citizens who
enjoy the protection of a government should contribute
their share of the cost of maintaining it, taxation requires
the consent of the taxpayers. 'For if any one shall claim a
power to lay and levy taxes on the people, by his own

[1] For further details about theories of property cf. O. Gierke, *Natural Law
and the Theory of Society* (tr. E. Barker, Cambridge, 1934), i. 104, ii. 295.
[2] *Second Treatise*, § 139.

authority, and without such consent by the people, he thereby invades the fundamental law of property, and subverts the end of government.'[1] The necessary consent, it turns out, may be only the consent of a majority, or it may be given indirectly, through representatives; but though these qualifications impair the consistency of Locke's theory, his main emphasis is not so much on the powers of government as on the necessity for consent of some kind.[2] And a markedly individualist tone is imparted to the whole of Locke's theory of property by his famous assumption that 'every man has a property in his own person: this nobody has any right to but himself. The labour of his body and the work of his hands we may say are properly his.'[3]

That Locke's theory of property had these characteristic features is not to be denied, and in this respect his attitude to property reflected an outlook common among men of his age. In the Middle Ages property had been conceived of in a more social and less individualist sense than was generally the case by the seventeenth century. Such notions as a just price, the condemnation of usury, and the

---

[1] *Second Treatise*, § 140.

[2] Sir Frederick Pollock pointed out that though Locke must have been familiar with the doctrine of eminent domain (*dominium eminens*), a widely current theory of medieval origin by which a right of individual property was combined with the overriding claims of the state, he nevertheless does not even mention it ('Locke's Theory of the State', in *Essays in the Law*, p. 91). It should be remembered, however, that eminent domain (on which see O. Gierke, *Political Theories of the Middle Age* (tr. F. W. Maitland, Cambridge, 1900), pp. 79, 178) was not known to English common law, which emphasized, on the contrary, the absolute character of rights of property. Locke was himself a close student of English political and constitutional tradition, in which the common law was an important element; he was writing for an English public, and he would naturally employ arguments to which the English ear was attuned. And, after all, he was writing to justify a curtailment, not an increase, of the arbitrary power of government.   [3] § 27.

principle of the general supremacy of natural law, implied some kind of check on the power of the property-owner to use his property as he liked. Already before Locke's time various factors—the breakdown of feudalism and the guild system, for example, and the growth of commercial capitalism as a consequence of the geographical discoveries and the economic expansion of the age of the Renaissance—had combined to destroy this medieval acceptance of social control. In England, moreover, it should be remembered that public opinion had become peculiarly sensitive to any attempt on the part of the government to raise taxes by unconstitutional means. Some of the major political disputes of the reigns of James I and Charles I had turned on fiscal questions, and these helped to make the sanctity of private property a political axiom to be defended to the uttermost against the pretensions of the royal prerogative. The same attitude persisted after the Restoration, and though the main counts against James II in the Declaration of Rights were concerned with other grievances, it was not for nothing that parliament inserted a formal statement of the established principle that money could not be levied 'by pretence of prerogative'. It is only to be expected, therefore, that a writer of Locke's day should give great prominence to the inviolability of private property. Nor was this principle peculiar to the Whigs; for the Tories, though in other respects they exalted the monarchy, held even stronger views than the Whigs on the importance of property, and particularly of property in land, which became a *sine qua non* for full citizenship.[1]

There is no reason to doubt that Locke shared this

[1] Only the owners of various kinds of real property could vote in parliamentary elections, and the Tories introduced legislation confining eligibility for membership of parliament to persons possessing an income from land.

outlook, but we should beware of exaggerating the extent of his individualism. In this, as in other parts of his political theory, he is providing a rational basis and explanation for current political beliefs and practices, and although the place he gives to the origins of private property in the state of nature, and his discussion of it in an early chapter, well before he comes to deal with the formation of civil society, are undoubtedly cardinal features of his system, we shall see, if we look more closely at this argument, that it is really less purely individualist than has sometimes been supposed. While propounding a theory of individual rights, he is at the same time continuing his attack on Sir Robert Filmer. Locke insists that God gave the world 'to Adam and his posterity in common', whereas according to Filmer God's gift was 'to Adam and his heirs in succession, exclusive of all the rest of his posterity'.[1] Locke had to reject this, as it was the basis of the divine-right monarchy affirmed by Filmer. Moreover, God gave men the faculty of reason that they might make use of the world 'to the best advantage of life and convenience'. Of course, before the fruits of the earth, and the beasts it feeds, which in their natural state are given to men in common, can benefit any particular man, 'there must of necessity be a means to appropriate them some way or other', and it is at this point that Locke introduces the notion that every man has a property in his own person, and consequently a right to make his own property whatever he has 'mixed his labour with' and so 'removed from the common state nature placed it in'. Critics have often attacked this notion, and pointed out various important reasons against its tenability as the foundation of a general theory of property. Sir Frederick Pollock, for example, complained that it is bad

---

[1] *Second Treatise*, § 25.

law,[1] and remarked that 'the rights of every man to personal safety, reputation, and so forth, are not marketable or transferable, and are wholly distinct in kind from rights of property. Locke's attempt to make an extended conception of Occupation bear the whole burden of Property was eminently that of an ingenious layman.'[2]

This was a characteristic lawyer's criticism, but it was a little less than fair to Locke. When he wrote that every man has a property in his own person, he was referring to men in the state of nature, not to citizens under government. This is perhaps to use the word property loosely, for the so-called property in his own person which Locke ascribes to a man is obviously not the same as the legally recognized property a citizen can have in land or movables. But Locke did not found the complete civic right of property solely upon this 'property' which each man has in his own person. It also rests on the law of nature, which 'willeth the peace and preservation of all mankind'.[3] This law can only be fulfilled, and God's bounty be made use of, if individuals can appropriate what they need, and notably the food required for survival. The labour of the individual, therefore, while a necessary stage, is only the final stage in the process of making property;[4] and, as Locke's eminently common-sense examples show, if there is a reasonable sense in which the contents of a man's stomach may be said to be his (though there is always something equivocal in the possessive pronoun), there is no logical point at which one can stop short of saying that the acorns or apples became his when he first gathered

---

[1] In Roman law also 'Dominus membrorum suorum nemo videtur' (*Digest*, IX. ii. 13).

[2] Sir F. Pollock, 'Locke's Theory of the State', in *Essays in the Law*, p. 90.

[3] *Second Treatise*, § 7.

[4] Cf. Willmoore Kendall, 'John Locke and the Doctrine of Majority-Rule' (*Illinois Studies in the Social Sciences*, xxvi, no. 2, 1941), p. 70.

them.[1] At this stage, in the state of nature, the dominant
consideration appears to be the common right of all, under
the law of nature, to preservation, for Locke proceeds to
tell us that a man may not 'engross as much as he will'. He
may only take what he can use 'before it spoils'. If he takes
more than this it is 'more than his share and belongs to
others'.[2] A man (in the state of nature) 'offended against
the common law of nature, and was liable to be punished'
if he took too much and allowed it to waste.[3] In these
passages Locke seems to think of property in terms of the
common advantage rather than of the private advantage
of the individual, and he remarks that when God gave the
world to mankind in common, he commanded man to
labour, 'to improve the earth for the benefit of life'.[4]
Mr. Kendall even declares that Locke's theory of property
is collectivist rather than individualist, and that he con-
ceives of the right of property simply as a function of a
man's duty to enrich man's common heritage.[5] This, however, is going too far, for in a later paragraph (to which
Mr. Kendall does not refer) Locke lays more emphasis on
the individual and less on the collective factor in the situa-

[1] The acorns may be derived from Pufendorf, according to whom nobody
owns the 'substances of things' in the state of nature, though their fruits can
be appropriated. Thus 'the acorns were his who took the pains of getting
them, but the oak had no particular owner' (*De Jure Naturae et Gentium*, IV. iv.
13). Locke's notion that 'this law of reason makes the deer that Indian's who
hath killed it' (§ 30), plausible as it sounds, is not necessarily true in fact of
primitive societies, which are often highly organized, and may insist on the
spoils of the chase being shared among the members of the tribe. His second
example is a better one, when he goes on to point out that even in civilized
communities, 'who have made and multiplied positive laws to determine
property', this 'original law of nature' still applies to sea-fishing, so that 'what
fish any one catches in the ocean, that great and still remaining common of
mankind . . . , is, by the labour that removes it out of that common state
nature left it in, made his property who takes that pains about it'.

[2] *Second Treatise*, § 31.

[3] § 37.   [4] § 32.

[5] Kendall, op. cit., pp. 71, 72.

tion.[1] Locke applies his labour principle not only to the fruits of the earth but also to the earth itself. 'As much land as a man tills, plants, improves, cultivates, and can use the product of, so much is his property. He by his labour does as it were enclose it from the common.'[2] Furthermore, though at first there are limits to what man may appropriate in the state of nature, Locke maintained that the introduction of money, which he ascribed to convention, made large-scale appropriation, hitherto physically impossible, both feasible and permissible, because money does not spoil, nor does the possession of it by one man lessen the stock of land or useful commodities available to others.[3] Obviously this nullifies the effectiveness of the limitation of private property in the common interest, and it has led Professor C. B. Macpherson to argue that this was the real point of Locke's theory.

Some writers have stressed the apparent moral inconsistency between Locke's limited right of appropriation in the state of nature and the unlimited property made possible by the invention of money, but we ought not to expect Locke or his contemporaries to have shared the outlook of a modern socialist. Professor Macpherson points out[4] that Locke seems to have thought that the state of nature could develop to a considerable degree of sophistication before political government was set up. Not only family relationships, including that between master and servant, 'came short of political society',[5] but money, and

[1] § 44: 'Though the things of nature are given in common, yet man, by being master of himself and proprietor of his own person and the actions and labour of it, had still in himself the great foundation of property.'

[2] § 32.   [3] §§ 36, 37, 50.

[4] C. B. Macpherson, 'Locke on Capitalist Appropriation', in *Western Political Quarterly*, iv (1951), pp. 550–66; 'The Social Bearing of Locke's Political Theory', ibid. vii (1954), pp. 1–22; *The Political Theory of Possessive Individualism* (Oxford, 1962), chapter v.

[5] *Second Treatise*, § 77.

labour hired for wages, had already come into existence in the state of nature. Macpherson argues that although at a primitive stage, when the acquisition of property meant little more than the collecting of food necessary to sustain life, the amount a man needed was limited, Locke deliberately intended to lead up to a justification of unlimited capitalist appropriation and the resultant unequal distribution of property. What made this possible, along with the invention of money, was the fact that he regarded labour as alienable property, which a man could sell for wages. This is why 'the turfs my servant has cut' become my property,[1] and not the servant's.

We may perhaps feel that this makes Locke's state of nature more unreal and incredible than ever, and wonder whether he really believed that a sophisticated commercial economy could exist, without any political government, in the state of nature. Macpherson replies that 'Locke's state of nature is a curious mixture of historical imagination and logical abstraction from civil society. Historically, a commercial economy without civil society is indeed improbable. But as an abstraction it is readily conceivable.'[2] Possibly; but this is not all. We are to understand that Locke set out to justify the unequal political and social structure consequent upon the development of capitalism. Only property-owners were fully members of the community, and this is why Locke thought that the sons of property-owners must give their consent to government as a condition of inheriting their fathers' property. Landless labourers, on the other hand, though necessary to the

[1] *Second Treatise*, § 23. As Mr. Laslett points out (Locke's *Two Treatises of Government* (Cambridge, 1960), p. 307, n.), this example, taken from the custom of the manor in an established community, is a bad illustration of appropriation in the state of nature, though it shows that Locke wished 'to explain himself in terms familiar to his readers'.

[2] *The Political Theory of Possessive Individualism*, p. 209.

community, were not full members of it, so that their consent was not needed. In any case they were so fully occupied with the struggle for a bare subsistence that they could not be expected to exercise or even possess a rational faculty. They could be relegated to the care of the poor law, and kept in a condition of due subservience by being offered a simplified form of religious belief 'suited to vulgar capacities'.[1]

This Marxist analysis undoubtedly puts Locke under a sharper light than some of the more traditional interpretations of his significance. But was all this really Locke's primary intention in writing? Doubtless he took for granted the existing capitalist structure of society. We may agree that he wished to provide a rational explanation of how it could have come into existence. But this is not to say that he entirely approved of it,[2] certainly not that his primary aim was to justify it, or that his great achievement was to have thought out an ingenious way of doing so. Nor was Locke's simplified religion intended as an opiate for the labouring masses. He was offering it to all alike, perhaps rather naïvely in modern eyes, but as a religious man himself, in the hope that it might help them. So again with the point about sons inheriting property. All Locke is saying, very reasonably, is that if sons wish to inherit property they must accept the conditions on which their fathers held it. He is not denying membership of the community to people who are not property-owners, even though they will admittedly be only second-class citizens, not possessing a vote at parliamentary elections. Locke after all was not only not a socialist. Neither was he a

[1] Ibid., p. 224.

[2] In § 111 he wrote of men's minds being corrupted by 'vain ambition, and *amor sceleratus habendi*, evil concupiscence'. This was one reason why it became necessary to establish civil government.

radical or a democrat, and he did not question the commonly held view that political power should be confined to people who had 'a stake in the country', or, as Ireton had said in the Putney debates, 'a permanent fixed interest in this kingdom'.[1]

Many Englishmen in the seventeenth century believed, like Locke, that the protection of property was the chief, if not the whole, business of the state.[2] Maximilian Petty upheld this view in the Putney debates,[3] and the eighth commandment was often cited as an argument that property was sanctioned by God and therefore natural.[4] Similarly, Locke's derivation of property from occupation was not, as Pollock thought, his own ingenious invention, but can be paralleled, like the other elements in his political theory, in the writings of numerous predecessors and contemporaries. James Tyrrell, for example, propounded a similar theory in *Patriarcha non Monarcha*, a reply to Filmer which he published in 1681. Earlier than this, Richard Baxter had held that 'each man hath that propriety in his life and faculties, and children, and estate and honour, that no rulers may unjustly take these from him'. Baxter went on, however, to attribute this right partly to

[1] A. S. P. Woodhouse, *Puritanism and Liberty* (1938), p. 54.

[2] The same belief may also be found in Locke's French Huguenot contemporary Pierre Jurieu, with whose thought he had some close affinities. See R. Lureau, *Les Doctrines politiques de Jurieu* (Bordeaux, 1904), p. 95, and G. H. Dodge, *The Political Theory of the Huguenots of the Dispersion* (New York, 1947), pp. 44 ff.

[3] A. S. P. Woodhouse, op. cit., p. 62.

[4] So Col. Rainborough in the Putney debates: Woodhouse, op. cit., p. 59. A typical and fairly readily accessible example of seventeenth-century views about property in England may be found in *An Argument for Self-Defence*, in *Somers Tracts*, ed. W. Scott, x. 278. This tract, according to a statement added to its title, was written about 1687, though not published until later. It echoes Locke at several points, declaring, for instance, that laws were ordained by general consent and for the public good, and that people entered society 'the better to be preserved in their lives and properties'.

the law of nature and 'other laws or institutions of God', but partly also to 'the specifying fundamental contracts of the commonwealth'.[1] Here he seems to waver between Locke's theory that property exists independently of the state, and the more usual theory that it was the result of convention. The latter theory also, however, found the ultimate origin of property in occupation, and the difference between this and Locke's theory reduces itself, upon analysis, to a question of the precise definition of *property*. The point is well brought out by Blackstone, who accepted Locke's ideas about the effect of labour. 'Bodily labour bestowed on any subject which before lay common to all men', he wrote, is 'universally allowed to give the fairest and most reasonable title to an exclusive property therein.' He then discussed the question how a permanent property in land could be acquired in this way.

Occupancy gave the right to the temporary *use* of the soil, so it is agreed upon all hands that occupancy gave also the original right to the permanent property in the substance of the earth itself. . . . There is indeed some difference of opinion among writers on natural law, concerning the reason why occupancy should convey this right . . .: Grotius and Puffendorf insisting that this right of occupancy is founded upon a tacit and implied assent of all mankind, that the first occupant should become the owner; . . . Mr. Locke, and others, holding that there is no such implied assent, neither is it necessary that there should be: for that the very act of occupancy, alone, being a degree of bodily labour, is from a principle of natural justice, without any consent or compact, sufficient of itself to gain a title.[2]

Critics of Locke have seen a difference in principle between mere occupation and a genuine *right* of property;

---

[1] R. Baxter, *A Holy Commonwealth* (1659), p. 69.
[2] W. Blackstone, *Commentaries*, ii. 1.

but Locke could believe that property in the strict sense existed in the state of nature, independently of government and civil society, because he thought of the state of nature as social and of the law of nature as a genuine law.

Locke's theory of labour as the origin of the right of property[1] leads to the labour theory of value. It is labour, he declares, that 'puts the difference of value on everything'. Land cultivated and planted is worth more than unimproved waste land, largely because of the effects of labour, and the same principle, he argues, applies to commodities like bread, wine, and cloth or silk (in comparison with acorns, water, and leaves, skin, or moss), as well as to the land itself.[2] Locke draws no distinction between a right to take the products of the earth and a right, by enclosure and tillage, to appropriate part of the earth itself. This, he argues, injured no one in the earliest times, when the population was small and the area of waste land available so huge that whatever one man took, there was still 'enough and as good' left over for others. Even in his own time, Locke thought, this condition still existed in the vast spaces of America, and, as he vividly puts it, 'in the beginning all the world was America'.[3] The labour theory of value was repeated by numerous eighteenth-century writers, so that it became a commonplace of economic

[1] I call the theory Locke's, but like the rest of his system it can be found in a number of earlier writers, among them Hobbes. Although, like Rousseau, Hobbes regarded legal property as the creation of the sovereign power of the state, it was based on what he called 'the plenty of matter', which 'God . . . either freely giveth, or for labour selleth to mankind. . . . Plenty dependeth (next to God's favour) meerly on the labour and industry of men' (*Leviathan*, c. 24). The labour theory of value was also upheld by Sir William Petty, who was a friend of Locke's. See his *Treatise of Taxes* (1662), where he remarks that 'all things ought to be valued by two natural Denominations. . . . Land and Labour' (*Works*, 1899 edn., i. 44).

[2] *Second Treatise*, §§ 40–4.

[3] § 49.

theory,[1] but it has been pointed out that Locke failed to discriminate between capitalist labour and wage-labour. He was aware that the labour which goes to the making of a commodity may have been contributed by a multiplicity of persons,[2] but he was thinking primarily of proprietors who owned the land they cultivated or the materials and tools of their trade, and made no distinction between their labour and that of their employees. Later writers were guilty of the same confusion, and when Ricardo distinguished floating capital, by which he meant the labour of wage-earners, or cattle, from fixed capital, the ultimate result was that in its latest guise, in socialist writers of the nineteenth century, the labour theory of value was transformed into something very different from what it had meant to Locke.[3] The wage-earning labourer now came to be thought of as the only real producer, while the capitalist was merely a non-productive lender of the means of production to the wage-earner.[4] Moreover, to Ricardo and his successors in the nineteenth century, value meant value in exchange, whereas for Locke (as for Aristotle and many other early economists) value was value for use.[5]

While Locke conceived of a necessary limitation to the acquisition of property in a primitive state of nature, he thought, as we have seen, that the invention of money allowed large accumulations of property to be made, and he did not question the unequal distribution of property that prevailed in his own time.[6] Within the state, in fact,

[1] Thus Adam Smith wrote that 'the property which every man has in his own labour, as it is the original foundation of all other property, so it is the most sacred and inviolable' (*Wealth of Nations*, I. x, pt. 2).

[2] Cf. his brief discussion of the various factors in the making of a loaf of bread (§ 43).

[3] Radicals and socialists used it to advocate the confiscation by the state of all incomes not clearly the reward of labour.

[4] Cf. M. Beer, *History of British Socialism* (1929 edn.), i. 192–7.

[5] *Second Treatise*, § 37.   [6] § 50.

citizens could legitimately expect the force of government to be used to protect whatever property they owned, and it was therefore the duty of government to provide this protection, and not to 'endeavour to take away or destroy the property of the people or reduce them to slavery under arbitrary power'.[1] Locke indeed declared that 'it is the duty of the civil magistrate, by impartially enacted equal laws, to preserve and secure for all the people in general, and for every one of his subjects in particular, the just possession of these things that belong to this life', by which he meant 'lands, money, houses, furniture, and the like'.[2] He also said that laws are made 'and rules set, as guards and defences to the properties of all the members of the society, to limit the power and moderate the dominion of every part and member of the society'.[3] Nevertheless, he did not stress the implications of such passages as these. The chief danger to be guarded against, as it seemed to him and his contemporaries, was interference with the liberty and property of the citizen by governments pretending to arbitrary power, and this may sufficiently explain why he dwelt more on the rights than on the duties involved in the possession of property.[4]

Locke, however, was not an advocate of *laissez-faire*, nor did he believe, as many early nineteenth-century economists did, that economic relationships would automatically balance and adjust themselves. He was a mercantilist, and believed in the regulation of trade. May be he did not realize what inordinate power the possession of great wealth can give, and if he had perhaps he would not have placed

[1] *Second Treatise*, § 222.
[2] *A Letter on Toleration* (ed. Klibansky and Gough (Oxford, 1968)), p. 67.
[3] *Second Treatise*, § 222.
[4] Cf. P. Larkin, *Property in the Eighteenth Century* (Cork, 1930), esp. pp. 78–90. For some correction of Larkin's work, cf. W. H. Hamilton's article on 'Property—according to Locke', in *Yale Law Journal*, xli (1931–2), pp. 864 ff.

political control in the hands of a property-owning
minority and expected them to exercise it impartially in
the interests of all. But if in this respect his political theory
strikes us as naïve and inadequate, it was at any rate no
more so than that of his contemporaries. It was not till
the age of the Industrial Revolution that men began to be
driven to change their views on the economic structure of
society, and even then many did so only very slowly and
reluctantly. It is true that, a generation before Locke,
there had been a few isolated thinkers who foreshadowed
a more modern outlook: Harrington,[1] for instance, who
had realized that political power is a function of economic
power, and Levellers like Rainborough, who had championed the claim of the poor man to equal treatment with
the well-to-do. But the nineteenth century had run more
than half its course before the importance of the economic
factor in politics began to be generally apprehended, and
it is foolish to blame Locke for not anticipating Karl
Marx. Locke may more fairly be blamed for the damage
he caused to his own reputation in later years by the loose
way in which he used the word 'property'. He repeatedly
declared that men entered civil society in order to protect
their property,[2] and defined political power, in the
opening chapter of the *Second Treatise*, as 'a right of making

[1] In *Oceana* (1656).

[2] Cf. § 124: 'The great and chief end . . . of men's uniting into commonwealths, and putting themselves under government, is the preservation of
property'; § 134: 'The great end of men's entering into society being the
enjoyment of their properties in peace and safety'; § 222: 'The reason why
men enter into society is the preservation of their property.' In § 94 he even
says that 'government has no other end but the preservation of property'.
This became almost an axiom of eighteenth-century political theory. It was
endorsed by Blackstone and repeated in legal judgements; Lord Camden,
for instance, made it the foundation of his decision in the famous case of
Entick *v.* Carrington (1765), and declared: 'The great end, for which men
entered society, was to secure their property. That right is preserved sacred
and incommunicable in all instances, where it has not been taken away or

laws . . . for the regulating and preserving of property'.[1]
But he included in 'the general name, property', every
man's 'life, liberty and estate',[2] that is, the whole of his
natural rights as a human being, and not simply his lands
and goods.[3] The narrow Whig view which made the
preservation of property in its ordinary restricted sense the
whole *raison d'être* of the state is really, therefore, a caricature of Locke, but he himself was partly responsible for
such a caricature gaining currency, because he often used
the word property in its ordinary sense; and it would not
be unfair to say that he gave the right of property in this
sense special prominence among the natural rights of man.
Chapter V of the *Second Treatise*, 'Of Property', is devoted
entirely to property in the narrower sense, and it is not
surprising, therefore, if eighteenth-century thinkers paid it
exclusive attention.

Among the natural rights with which everyone was born
Locke included 'a right, before any other man, to inherit
with his brethren his father's goods'. He coupled this with
'a right of freedom to his person, which no other man has
a power over, but the free disposal of it lies in himself'.[4]
Locke seems to have thought of these two rights as essentially connected, and the result is that one may counteract
the other, and prevent the effective enjoyment of both.
Thus, 'a man is naturally free from subjection to any
government, though he be born in a place under its jurisdiction', and if he chooses he may 'disclaim the lawful

abridged by some public law for the good of the whole.' (C. Grant Robertson, *Select Statutes, Cases and Documents*, p. 465.)

[1] *Second Treatise*, § 3.

[2] §§ 123, 87.

[3] In § 131 man enters civil society 'the better to preserve himself, his
liberty and property'.

[4] § 190. The eldest son, it will be observed, has no priority by natural law,
nor does Locke pretend that testamentary bequest is a natural right.

government of the country he was born in'; but if he makes this choice 'he must also quit the right that belonged to him by the laws of it and the possessions there descending to him from his ancestors, if it were a government made by their consent'.[1]

Locke's belief in the inviolability of property is nowhere more forcibly illustrated than in his theory of the rights of conquest. Consent being the only legitimate basis of government, no right of government can be founded on mere success in an unjust and aggressive war; and even in a lawful war the conqueror by virtue of his conquest acquires no rights over his own supporters. Furthermore, though a lawful conqueror acquires despotic power over the conquered, there are strict limits to this power. 'He has an absolute power over the lives of those who by an unjust war (sc. in resisting his conquest) have forfeited them; but not over the lives and fortunes of those who engaged not in the war, nor over the possessions even of those who were actually engaged in it.'[2] Locke explains at some length his doctrine that conquest conveys no title to the possessions of the conquered. The life of the conquered may be forfeit, but his goods, on the principle that nature 'willeth the preservation of all mankind as much as possible', are intended by nature 'to belong to the children to keep them from perishing', and so, in spite of the conquest, they 'do still continue to belong to his children'. The most that can be exacted from the land of the conquered is 'reparation for the damages received and the charges of the war, and that too with reservation of the right of the innocent wife and children';[3] and even this reparation turns out to be

[1] § 191. Cf. § 73.
[2] § 178. On this last point see the next paragraph.
[3] § 182. Similarly, Locke argues, 'I may kill a thief that sets on me in the highway, yet I may not . . . take away his money . . .; this would be robbery on my side.'

severely restricted. Money, according to Locke, has only conventional value (men 'agreed that a little piece of yellow metal which would keep without wasting or decay should be worth a great piece of flesh or a whole heap of corn'),[1] and so he now proceeds to strike out of the bill 'money and such riches, and treasure taken away', because 'these are none of nature's goods, they have but a fantastical imaginary value: nature hath put no such upon them. They are of no more account by her standard than the wampompeke of the Americans to a European prince.'[2] Only the land itself is to be considered, and the damage caused by war, he argues, will amount only to 'a year's product or two', and 'seldom reaches four or five', so that the actual annexation of a conquered country can never be justified. Locke therefore concludes that when a people have been conquered and forced to submit to a government 'against their free consents', their descendants retain a right to the estates of their ancestors, and are entitled, 'whenever they have a power to do it', to overthrow an alien government and regain the lands their ancestors once held. Thus the 'Grecian Christians . . . may justly cast off the Turkish yoke, which they have so long groaned under', because they are 'descendants of the ancient possessors of that country'.[3]

Locke expected his limitation of the rights of conquerors to seem 'a strange doctrine, it being so quite contrary to the practice of the world; there being nothing more familiar in

---

[1] *Second Treatise*, § 37.

[2] § 184. The reason, no doubt, for this astonishing argument is that, as mentioned above (p. 93), Locke meant by value intrinsic and not exchange value. Even so, of course, he is quite wrong about the nature of gold. We may respect Locke's hatred of war and his consequent desire to minimize the claims of conquerors, but his good feelings have got the better of his judgement.

[3] § 192.

speaking of the dominion of countries, than to say such a one conquered it'.[1] On the contrary, international law has come to recognize the rights of private property in war, for even though it may be impossible for owners of property to continue to enjoy their rights in a country under enemy occupation, these rights are not nullified thereby, but may be resumed on the restoration of peace, and an occupying power may establish a 'custodian of enemy property' in conquered territory to safeguard the interests of the owners. Locke's error is in failing to differentiate between the right of an individual to his property and the claim of a government to found political power on conquest. We should not be surprised at this, for the political thought of his age did not clearly distinguish between them.[2] Absolute monarchs like Louis XIV, for instance, claimed to inherit provinces and kingdoms (and to rule over their inhabitants) just as if they were the private estates of an ordinary individual. The patriarchal theory of the origin of monarchical authority rested on the same confusion, and found acceptance because many of the ideas of feudal society (in which the private and the political aspects of land tenure were essentially blended) still held the field. Even in England, where royal absolutism had been checked, and parliament was beginning to share the responsibility of government, the persistence of the notion that the king should 'live of his own' indicated the survival of some of the old ideas. Locke rejected

[1] § 180.

[2] Perhaps it would be fairer to say that political practice did not distinguish, for lawyers had long marked the difference. Cf. Gierke, *Natural Law and the Theory of Society* (tr. E. Barker), i. 162, and his apt anecdote of the two lawyers who were asked by the Emperor Frederick I whether he had *dominium* as well as *imperium* over his subjects' lands. One said he had, and was rewarded with the gift of a horse, whereupon the other commented: 'Amisi equum quia dixi aequum.'

Filmer's theory that kings derive their titles by inheritance from Adam, but confusion between the property-rights of individuals and the political powers of governments may be partly due to the belief that political power is derived from the consents of individuals.

It is, in fact, this belief, or at any rate the form in which he stated it, that lies at the root of many of the difficulties in Locke's whole theory of property. His theory of property, like his theory of government, is vitiated by being stated in terms of an antecedent, quasi-historical state of nature, in which men actually enjoyed and exercised their natural rights. It is this quasi-historicity of the state of nature which leads him to base property on appropriation, and to equate this with the exercise of a right. In this respect, at any rate, Rousseau's theory of property was sounder than Locke's. Rousseau carefully distinguished between a mere fact (such as the exercise of force, which is the basis of appropriation in the state of nature) and a right,[1] 'between possessions which derive from physical strength and the right of the first comer, and ownership which can be based only on a positive title'.[2] Rousseau's system, it is true, like Locke's, also contains a quasi-historical state of nature and a social contract to transform it into political society, but all this was only the form in which he stated his doctrine, and he was not interested in the question whether it had ever actually happened. Locke, on the other hand, and his Whig contemporaries, seem to have believed that the social contract was an historical fact, and that every individual citizen gave his personal consent to government, either then or subsequently, even though he may have given it tacitly. Locke recognized that, within the state, property was held on conditions regulated by positive law, but, still clinging to the notion that the right of

[1] *Contrat Social*, i. 3.   [2] Ibid. i. 8.

property was sacred and could not be invaded without the consent of the owner, he insisted that there could be no legitimate taxation except by consent. As we have seen, he equated this with what later became the famous slogan of the American colonists, 'no taxation without representation', but only at the cost of weakening the effectiveness of individual consent.[1] Rousseau had no such qualms. There could be no genuine right of property, as distinct from mere precarious possession, except in the state. Property must therefore be held on whatever conditions the state imposes, which means, in effect, that the individual must submit to the direction of the general will in matters of property as in everything else. Though Locke's *Treatise* contains passages which appear to anticipate Rousseau's position,[2] he lays his main emphasis on the rights of men. He often does so, it must be admitted, at the cost of consistency, but we may conclude that even though Locke's theory is ultimately illogical, if all its implications are pressed, its practical effects are more tolerable than the totalitarian absolutism which results from a ruthless pursuit of Rousseau's doctrine to its logical conclusion.

[1] Mr. A. H. Maclean, of Peterhouse, Cambridge, in a doctoral thesis on *The Origins of the Political Opinions of John Locke*, has suggested that though Locke was prepared to allow taxation to be levied by the decision of a majority, this is as far as he would have gone, and he would have required strictly individual consent to justify any other kind of interference with private property. I should be inclined to agree. The effect of this doctrine in America was, of course, a demand not for more effective representation, but that the unrepresented should not be taxed. The theory of property common in the eighteenth century is reflected in the preference for indirect rather than direct taxation, on the ground that (provided necessaries were not taxed) the purchaser of taxed articles voluntarily taxed himself. One of the objections raised against Pitt's income tax in 1799 was that it sacrificed 'optionality', which was the 'very essence of taxation in a free country'. A compulsory tax which none could avoid threatened 'the dominion of property' (cf. P. Larkin, op. cit., pp. 115–18).

[2] Cf. p. 36, above.

It is interesting to notice that the liberal reaction in recent times against the absolutist claims of a dictatorial state has led to a restatement of the once apparently discredited notion of the rights of man, or natural rights. And among these rights we may even find once more a right of property.[1] It is possible to maintain that there is a natural right of property which the state should respect, in the sense that property is a (morally) desirable institution, and that it is right that the state should be so organized as to enable its citizens to own property. It is possible, and indeed essential, to combine such a belief with the belief that the state should also impose regulations and conditions to prevent the abuse of property. Such a natural right of property is to be distinguished from Locke's natural right to appropriate and own particular pieces of property, and its foundation will not be (as in Locke) the mere fact of having appropriated them. If a natural right of property is to be admitted, it must rest on the same kind of grounds as those on which liberty also may be defended as a natural right. This will be no 'absolute' right for the individual to own, or to act, regardless of his neighbours. It will operate essentially within and be conditioned by its social setting. One may maintain that without such rights the life of society, and of the individuals of whom society is composed, is impoverished, and lacks a condition essential to the full development of personality.[2] In this, as in other aspects of

[1] Long before the latter-day reaction against totalitarianism, papal political theory insisted on natural rights, including a natural right of property. At the same time it repudiated 'liberalism', i.e. the doctrines of the sovereignty of the people, and similar products of the French Revolution; but we may observe that the basis of these natural rights is essentially the same as what Locke meant by natural law, namely, God's will as the rational determinant of all human affairs. Cf. the Encyclicals *Rerum Novarum* (published by Leo XIII in 1891) and *Quadragesimo Anno* (published by Pius XI in 1931).

[2] Cf. Aristotle's defence of private property against common ownership in *Politics*, book II, esp. c. v, § 8 (1263 *b*).

his political thought, we may feel that Locke reached the right conclusions, even though his reasoning was faulty and his route confused, and we may be thankful that his sane moderation, even if it was based on too sanguine a belief in the reasonableness of mankind, has characterized much of our constitutional development.

V

THE SEPARATION OF POWERS
AND SOVEREIGNTY

THE invention of the doctrine of the separation of powers
has often been attributed to Montesquieu, and a number
of critics have stressed the originality and independence of
his contribution in this respect to political science.[1] As
long ago as 1836, however, a German writer, Carl Ernst
Jarcke, detected in Locke the originator of the doctrine of
the separation and balance of powers, and, regarding this
as an absurd and impossible account of the English constitution, branded him as 'the creator of the false theory of
the English state'.[2] This verdict was accepted by Teich-
müller, in reply to whom yet another scholar, Harry
Janssen, while agreeing that Montesquieu was not entitled
to the credit of originating the famous doctrine, also denied
Locke's claim to have discovered it, and ingeniously
ascribed 'the real revelation of the secret of English

[1] e.g. Robert von Mohl, Bluntschli, and others. In this country Leslie
Stephen remarked only that the separation of powers in Locke 'may remind
us of Montesquieu' (*English Thought in the Eighteenth Century*, ii. 143). In
The Evolution of Parliament (1920), c. xii, A. F. Pollard, while castigating the
notion that the separation of powers is to be found in the English constitution, blamed Montesquieu and no one else for first being deceived into
seeing it there.

[2] In *Die Ursprünge des modernen Constitutionalismus*. In an edition of Montesquieu's works published at Paris in 1839 the editor, M. Parelle, remarked in
a footnote to the chapter 'De la Constitution de l'Angleterre' (*De l'Esprit des
Lois*, xi. 6), which contains Montesquieu's account of the doctrine: 'La
plupart des principes que Montesquieu pose dans ce chapitre sont tirés du
Traité de Gouvernement civil, de Locke.'

constitutionalism' to Swift's *Discourse of the Contests and Dissensions between the Nobles and the Commons in Athens and Rome*. It was not difficult to point out that this latter attribution could not be accepted, for Montesquieu's three powers, legislative, executive, and judicial, are distinguished by function, whereas Swift found the key to the constitution in the interaction and balance of king, lords, and commons. Though the powers mentioned by Locke diverge somewhat in function and nomenclature from those in Montesquieu, and the two writers differed in their approach, yet in principle a parallel could be established between them.[1] It seemed, then, that Jarcke's verdict was substantially correct after all.

This, however, is not the end of the story, for M. Dedieu pointed out[2] that while Montesquieu's cardinal principle is, or purports to be[3] to guarantee political liberty, and make despotism impossible, by a complete and absolute separation of powers, each of the three functions of government being entrusted to persons or bodies who must be kept distinct and independent of each other, Locke, after enumerating his three powers, does not keep them rigidly separate and independent, but expressly stresses the supremacy of the legislature. Furthermore, Montesquieu's principle of the separation of the legislative, executive, and judicial functions was associated in his political theory with another principle—the combination of the three traditional forms of government, monarchy, aristocracy, and democracy. The peculiar merit of English parliamentary government, as he saw it in the eighteenth century, was its happy fusion of these two principles. The separation of

[1] T. Pietsch, *Über das Verhältniss der politischen Theorie Lockes zu Montesquieus Lehre von der Theilung der Gewalten* (Breslau, 1887), pp. 3–9.

[2] J. Dedieu, *Montesquieu et la tradition politique anglaise en France* (Paris, 1909), pp. 160–89.

[3] Cf. the next paragraph, below.

powers made arbitrary government impossible, while the combination of the forms of government preserved what was best in each. The essence of the English constitution, according to Montesquieu's account, therefore, consisted not only in the separation of the legislative, executive, and judicial powers, but in putting the executive in the hands of the monarch, entrusting the judicial and part of the legislative power to the aristocracy, while democracy had the remainder of the legislative power.[1]

The result of associating these two principles is that though Montesquieu opens his chapter by insisting that if any one of the three powers is combined with another, liberty will be destroyed, in practice the separation works out less rigidly. Thus he gives the executive a power of veto over the legislature, to prevent the latter becoming despotic, though he does not recommend that the legislature should have a similar control over the executive, nor that the monarch should exercise legislative power by prerogative. Moreover, he approves of the English arrangement by which the judicial power is exercised by 'la partie du corps législatif qui est composée de nobles'. Here he evidently has in mind the position of the House of Lords as the supreme court of appeal, for a couple of pages later he remarks that in general the judicial power should not be exercised by any part of the legislature, with three exceptions. One of these is appellate jurisdiction, and another the trial of peers, who, on account of popular envy,

[1] This is the substratum of truth beneath Janssen's theory, but there seems no reason to suppose that Montesquieu got it from Swift. Swift himself used language which he may have derived from Locke, for after stating at the outset that 'in all government there is an absolute power unlimited', which is 'placed fundamentally in the body of the people', he remarks that this is 'a trust too great to be committed to any one man or assembly', and 'mixed government' was therefore established (*Works*, 1897, edn., i. 231). Swift's *Discourse*, the first of his political writings, was published in 1701. On mixed government see below, p. 111.

may not get a fair trial before the ordinary tribunals. The third is impeachment, in which both houses of the legislature are concerned, the lower as accuser, the upper as judge. In this way, while the more faithfully describing the English constitution, Montesquieu obviously blurs the edges of his theoretical separation of powers. Writers who followed him, however, declared firmly that there could be no liberty unless the powers were kept separate, and the framers of the American constitution took care to ensure that this principle should be rigidly adhered to.[1]

How much did Montesquieu owe to Locke? To answer this question, let us turn once more to Locke, and remind ourselves of his teaching on this subject. 'The first and fundamental positive law of all commonwealths', he tells us, 'is the establishing of the legislative power', which will be 'not only the supreme power of the commonwealth but sacred and unalterable in the hands where the community have once placed it.'[2] The legislative body, however, need not be 'always in being', nor is it 'so much as convenient that it should be'[3] (and here Locke was echoing the attitude to parliament still usual in England, for nobody thought long and frequent sessions desirable),[4] whereas

[1] Cf. A. F. Pollard, *The Evolution of Parliament* (1920), pp. 235, 236.

[2] *Second Treatise*, § 134.

[3] § 153. Cf. § 156, where Locke recognizes that the need may arise to convene the legislature rapidly in an emergency, but thinks that 'constant frequent meetings . . . and long continuations of their assemblies . . . could not but be burthensome to the people, and must necessarily in time produce more dangerous inconveniences'.

[4] Cf. Cromwell's attack, in his speech of 12 Sept. 1654, on the notion that 'when one Parliament had left its seat another was to sit down immediately in the room thereof' (T. Carlyle, *O. Cromwell's Letters and Speeches*, ed. S. C. Lomas, ii. 370). He returned to the same theme on 21 April 1657, and went on to stress the danger of arbitrary power 'whilst the Legislative is perpetually exercised; when the Legislative and Executive Power are always the same. . . . And if they could make Laws and judge too, you would have excellent Laws!' (ibid. iii. 93).

'the laws that are at once and in a short time made have a constant and lasting force and need a perpetual execution or an attendance thereto'; therefore a continuous executive is necessary, 'and thus the legislative and executive power come often to be separated'.[1] The separation of these powers would seem, therefore, to be only a matter of convenience, and not a dogma emphasized by Locke as vitally important.[2] Locke goes farther than this, however, for he points out also that 'it may be too great a temptation to human frailty, apt to grasp at power, for the same persons, who have the power of making laws, to have also in their hands the power to execute them'. It is true that Locke does not go as far as Montesquieu and declare that if executive and legislative powers were in the same hands there could be no liberty, but he clearly believed it desirable to keep them separate.

Montesquieu's third power was the judicial, but Locke does not mention this specifically. He seems to include it in his executive power, which is concerned with the whole administration of the laws; and after all, in the seventeenth century, much of what we should regard as executive action was in fact performed by the courts of law, and by officers, such as the justices of the peace, whose functions were both executive and judicial. Instead of the judicature, Locke mentions a third power of his own, 'which may be called federative, if any one pleases', from the Latin *foedera*, for it deals with 'war and peace, leagues and alliances'. So far from stressing the separateness of this third power, however, Locke tells us that though the executive and federative powers 'be really distinct in themselves, yet they are hardly to be separated and placed at

[1] *Second Treatise*, §§ 143, 144.
[2] Cf. E. Barker's Introduction to his *Social Contract* (Oxford, 1947), pp. xxvii n., xxviii.

the same time in the hands of distinct persons'.[1] The upshot is, therefore, that Locke's system contains only two really separate powers, the legislative and the combined executive-federative-judicial. This seems to rule out the thesis that Montesquieu borrowed his doctrine from Locke; but closer examination of Montesquieu reveals that in substance he is closer to Locke than appears at first sight. The opening sentence of Montesquieu's chapter distinguishes 'trois sortes de pouvoirs'. The first is 'la puissance législative', and the second 'la puissance exécutrice des choses qui dépendent du droit des gens', which corresponds with Locke's federative power. The third is 'la puissance exécutrice de celles qui dépendent du droit civil', which 'punit les crimes ou juge les différends des particuliers'. Montesquieu adds that he will call this third power judicial, and the second 'simplement la puissance exécutrice de l'état'. Montesquieu does not, it is true, suggest that his second and third powers are usually in the same hands, but his judicial power is confused with what would nowadays be called the executive, in much the same way as in Locke, and he also remarks that it is 'en quelque façon nulle'. As far as this point goes, therefore, the clear distinction often drawn between Montesquieu and Locke falls to the ground. A more valid and fundamental difference between the two may be detected in the fact that Montesquieu's theory was that in a free state there was to be no sovereign power, but the government must consist of separate bodies parallel and equal in authority; whereas Locke ascribed to the legislative a supremacy over the others. According to M. Dedieu, however, Locke never meant his legislative power to be sovereign. Sovereignty belongs to the people who erected the legislature, and M. Dedieu's conclusion, therefore, was that the

[1] §§ 145–8.

similarities outweigh the differences between Montesquieu and Locke, and that Montesquieu in effect only perfected a constitutional model which was really derived from Locke.[1]

Let us leave the question of sovereignty for the moment, and consider whether the model which Montesquieu 'perfected' was really Locke's. It may be true that Montesquieu derived some of his ideas from Locke, but he may equally well have formulated his theories as a result of his own observation of the English constitution, as indeed Locke himself may have done. Dr. Robert Shackleton has argued persuasively that the immediate source of Montesquieu's doctrine was Bolingbroke, who in his efforts to undermine Walpole's ascendancy in parliament was carrying on an active campaign in *The Craftsman* for the separation of powers at the time of Montesquieu's visit to England in 1730.[2] Montesquieu elevated Bolingbroke's political propaganda into a constitutional theory; but he may still, at one remove, have been indebted for it to Locke, for Bolingbroke himself echoed some of Locke's ideas.[3] One thing which is certain is that the theory was not new in Locke's time any more than it was in Montesquieu's. Like practically every feature in Locke's political system, it was widely current in English political thought; and this is not surprising, for it corresponded with the operation of the English constitution as then generally understood. In view

[1] J. Dedieu, op. cit., pp. 181 ff.

[2] R. Shackleton, 'Montesquieu, Bolingbroke, and the Separation of Powers', in *French Studies*, iii (1949), pp. 25 ff., 33–8. Cf. also his *Montesquieu, a Critical Biography* (Oxford, 1961), pp. 298–301.

[3] He denied the power of parliament to 'annul the constitution', and ascribed to the legislature 'a supreme, and . . . in one sense an absolute, but in none an arbitrary power. It is limited to the public good of the society', and in the last resort, in case of abuse, the people have a right of resistance. This is obviously pure Locke (Bolingbroke, *Dissertation of Parties* (1773–4), Letter xvii).

of the contest for power between king and parliament, which was the dominant feature of English history in the seventeenth century, and the constant efforts of parliament to check and oppose the actions of the king and his ministers, the distinction between executive and legislature was an obvious one, and it can be found in a number of writers before the publication of Locke's *Treatises*. Equally obvious was the separation of the judicial power. All through the seventeenth century the commons charged the judges with subservience to royal influence, and in order to secure their independence insisted that they should be appointed *quamdiu se bene gesserint* instead of *durante beneplacito regis*— a point which was won at last in the Act of Settlement (1701).

Although they were really inconsistent, the principle of the separation of powers was not infrequently combined with the idea that the best safeguard against arbitrary government was a system of 'checks and balances' embodied in a 'mixed' constitution. The idea that features of the 'simple' forms of government could be combined or mixed goes back to Aristotle and Polybius, and in the seventeenth century it became a commonplace to interpret the English constitution as a mixture of monarchy, aristocracy, and democracy. The idea that the English monarchy was a mixed monarchy was given prominence by its adoption in 1642 by the authors of the king's Answer to the Nineteen Propositions submitted to him by parliament, and from then onwards a whole series of political writers repeatedly maintained the thesis that the peculiar virtue of the English constitution lay in its balance or mixture.[1] In spite of a superficial resemblance this principle was not the same as the separation of powers. A mixed

[1] For a detailed demonstration of this see C. C. Weston, *English Constitutional Theory and the House of Lords* (1965).

government was consistent with the principle of legislative sovereignty, held jointly by king, lords, and commons, whereas the separation of powers was specifically designed, by setting one power against another, to make sovereignty impossible.[1] But in a mixed government, sovereignty could only be exercised effectively when the component elements co-operated; when, as happened in the seventeenth century, they disagreed, the effect was the same as that of a separation of powers, and may indeed have helped to generate the latter theory. Moreover, the principle of legislative sovereignty was imperfectly understood and established in seventeenth-century England, and this tended to conceal the difference between mixed government and the separation of powers.[2] Political writers, Bolingbroke among them, often combined the two, and Montesquieu himself, as we have been, blurred the sharp outlines of his theory of separation by associating with it some elements of the theory of mixture. Locke, on the other hand, though he did not use the word 'sovereign' to describe his legislative power, clearly recognized its 'supremacy'. Here again, as in other aspects of his political theory, Locke was not original, for even if the full implications of sovereignty (as enunciated, for instance, by Filmer and Hobbes) were not generally accepted, the claims of the legislature to supremacy had long been widely supported, and were reinforced by the policy of the Long Parliament and its exercise of power during the Civil War and the Commonwealth.

The distinction, if not the actual separation, of powers,

[1] It is worth noticing that for Locke and Montesquieu the important point was the separation of executive and legislature, whereas in the American constitution it is the separate judicial power which, as far as legislation is concerned, makes Congress a non-sovereign body.

[2] Cf. M. J. C. Vile, *Constitutionalism and the Separation of Powers* (Oxford, 1967), pp. 33–4, 54 ff.

combined with the supremacy of the legislature, are among the numerous features in which Locke's political system was anticipated a generation earlier by the Rev. George Lawson,[1] among others, and we may observe with interest that in this respect Lawson was clearer and more up to date than Locke, for the three powers he distinguished were the legislative, executive, and judicial, and he added that we should 'understand judicial and executive in a larger sense than they are commonly taken'. Jurisdiction includes not only judgement but the execution of judgement: the executive power does not execute the judge's sentence (that is a part of jurisdiction) but is something wider, and denotes everything that tends to the execution of the laws, including the appointment of all kinds of officers, civil and military, internal and external.[2] The only original point in Locke seems to be his use of the term federative; and that was the only point which was not adopted by other writers. It is clear, therefore, that neither Locke nor Montesquieu can claim to have actually originated the idea of the separation of powers, though no doubt the effective popularization of the theory was due much more to their work, and especially to Montesquieu's, than to the writings of earlier but obscurer authors whose existence was quickly forgotten.[3] Nevertheless, I think we should at any rate refrain from saying that Locke (or Montesquieu) was the 'creator' of the 'false theory of the English state'.

Was it, after all, a 'false theory?' A. F. Pollard admitted

[1] Cf. A. H. Maclean, 'George Lawson and John Locke', in *Cambridge Historical Journal*, ix, no. 1 (1947), pp. 69–77.

[2] G. Lawson, *Examination of the Political Part of Mr. Hobbes his Leviathan* (1657), p. 8; *Politica Sacra et Civilis* (1660), p. 41.

[3] Lawson's work, as a matter of fact, was reprinted at the time of the Revolution, as Mr. Maclean has pointed out. So was Philip Hunton's *Treatise of Monarchy* (first published in 1643), which advocated mixed monarchy, and various other tracts besides.

that the age of Montesquieu was the age of place bills, and that in its distrust of the crown and its desire to be independent parliament was deliberately aiming at a complete separation between executive and legislature. Montesquieu's mistake, he suggested, was in treating this aim as accomplished when in fact, though he failed to realize it, the growth of the cabinet was counteracting it, with the result that the essence of the modern constitution is that the powers are not separated but intimately linked together.[1] Is it fair, however, to expect Montesquieu (still less Locke and his predecessors in the seventeenth century), to have grasped the proleptic significance of the cabinet, which was still a semi-secret and irregular body,[2] when even as late as the middle of the nineteenth century Bagehot had to explain to his readers just how the cabinet made the English constitution differ from the American, and to point out why such time-honoured doctrines as the separation of powers and 'checks and balances' no longer provided the real explanation of how it works? More recently, indeed, Bagehot himself has been criticized for propagating a 'false theory' of the English constitution, describing the cabinet as 'a committee of the parliamentary majority', though he also recognized that the real essence of political life is 'the action and reaction between the Ministry and the Parliament'. Actually, as L. S. Amery pointed out, Montesquieu was not 'so wide of the mark as is sometimes thought when he made the division and equipoise of powers in our Constitution its chief characteristic and the secret of its success'.[3]

[1] A. F. Pollard, *The Evolution of Parliament* (1920), pp. 237, 238.

[2] Cf. the clauses in the Act of Settlement (1701) designed to force the taking of decisions in the Privy Council instead of in the still unofficial and unauthorized cabinet.

[3] Cf. W. Bagehot, *The English Constitution* (1867), c. i, *ad init.*; L. S. Amery, *Thoughts on the Constitution* (Oxford, 1947), c. 1.

In our modern government, subject to having the support of a majority in parliament, the cabinet wields the power of the crown. The constitution is, in fact, the lineal descendent of the medieval polity, in which, while there was a progressive differentiation of functions, every organ and institution had a common origin in the court and the authority of the king. Yet while the thread of the royal authority can be traced throughout our constitutional history, the constitution has never been a written one, and has always been subject to changes of direction. Earlier in the seventeenth century it might, had the efforts of parliament not been successful, have turned into a monarchical despotism of the continental type. Equally the efforts of parliament in the later seventeenth and early eighteenth centuries to ensure its independence of the crown by enforcing a separation of powers might conceivably have resulted in the establishment of an American type of government in England. Looked at in retrospect, in the light of a 'Whig interpretation of history', the modern constitution may seem to be the logical and natural product of its previous history, but it is surely irrational to maintain that it was always inevitable that it should develop in the direction it actually took. In the seventeenth century the constitution, though potentially a cabinet constitution, was actually not yet anything of the kind, and to describe it in nineteenth-century terms would be as misleading as to interpret the constitutional crises of the Middle Ages in terms of the seventeenth century. This is what the lawyers and politicians of that century were apt to do, but even though they were mistaken as historians, and their vision could not penetrate the future, I think we must credit them with some understanding of how the government worked in their own age. Let us turn, then, to Locke's theory of government, and I think we shall recognize in it a description, if in general terms, of the English constitution of his own day, which after all he had had good opportunity, through actual experience and long study, to get to know.

As we have seen, the first point he mentions is the establishment of the legislature, which is 'the supreme power of the commonwealth';[1] the executive 'is visibly subordinate and accountable to' the legislative power, 'and may be at pleasure changed and displaced';[2] but (with the English constitution obviously in mind, though he refers only to 'some commonwealths') the executive may be 'vested in a single person, who has also a share in the legislative', in which case 'that single person in a very tolerable sense may also be called supreme'.[3] This is not because he exercises the supreme power ('which is that of law-making') himself, but because he is supreme over all inferior executive magistrates, and also because he has no legislative superior, 'there being no law to be made without his consent'. He may also have the power of assembling and dismissing the legislature, but this 'gives not the executive a superiority over it, but is a fiduciary trust placed in him'.[4] In addition to these powers, Locke admits that 'the good of the society requires that several things should be left to the discretion of him that has the executive power', and 'this power to act according to discretion for the public good, without the prescription of the law, and sometimes even against it, is that which is called prerogative.'[5] In this chapter, where the very word prerogative must have evoked memories of recent constitutional disputes, Locke

[1] *Second Treatise*, § 134. I postpone discussion of the implications of this supremacy, and return to it on pp. 123 ff.

[2] § 152.   [3] § 151.   [4] § 156.

[5] §§ 159, 160. In § 210 prerogative, described as a trust, is even called 'an arbitrary power in some things left in the prince's hand'; but it is 'to do good, not harm to the people'.

practically drops any pretence of generality, and alludes openly to English history[1] and the king's 'power of calling parliaments in England, as to precise time, place, and duration'.[2]

If Locke's account of the English constitution is described as 'false', the charge against him is, presumably, that instead of recognizing the principle of sovereignty he conceived of the legislative power as limited, in that he insisted on the separation of powers, rather than on their union, through the cabinet, in parliament. Now if the framers of the American constitution, which embodied the doctrine of the separation of powers in an extreme form, imagined themselves to be copying the English model, they were obviously misled. The essence and intention of the American constitution was to allow no part of the government to be sovereign, but to ensure that each should limit and check the scope of the others. If Locke, even indirectly, were a source from which the Americans derived their theory of government,[3] he bears some degree of responsibility for its product, the American constitution. But the framers of the American constitution were not so much copying the English model as avoiding what they regarded as its defects. In particular, they were resisting the legal omnipotence of parliament, which had recently been displayed in the enactment of the Stamp Act and the Declaratory Act.[4]

This brings us to the question of sovereignty, and it would be as well to make clear at the outset that the

---

[1] § 165.   [2] § 167.

[3] Mr. John Dunn has argued that the extent of Locke's influence on the makers of the American constitution was much less than has often been supposed. See his 'The Politics of John Locke in England and America in the Eighteenth Century', in J. W. Yolton (ed.), *John Locke, Problems and Perspectives* (Cambridge, 1969), pp. 45–80.

[4] 5 Geo. III, c. 12; 6 Geo III, c. 12.

subject to be discussed is legislative sovereignty as a legal term, and not (to begin with at any rate) any question of the sovereignty of the people, or of the general will, in vaguer and non-technical senses of the word.[1] It is in the legal sense (as defined and explained, for example, in the well-known chapters in Dicey's *Law of the Constitution*) that we can say that the modern English constitution embodies the sovereignty of parliament, in contrast to the American constitution, in which congress it not a sovereign law-making body. It is in this legal sense, too, that Hobbes's sovereign fills the centre of his stage, though he also held the supreme executive authority. Hobbes's 'one man, or one assembly of men' possessed a legally unlimited power of making laws, which no other authority in the realm could challenge or set aside, and this is the essence of the legal sovereignty ascribed by Dicey to the modern parliament. Now, did Locke's theory recognize the existence of such a power?

It is clear that Locke definitely refused to allow anybody in his state, whether legislative or executive, to exercise unlimited power in the Hobbesian sense. He would have repudiated this as tyranny or 'arbitrary power', and every Englishman who prided himself on the English constitution would have agreed with him. Earlier in his life, however, it seems that Locke's attitude might have been different. His experiences during the Civil War and Interregnum made him welcome the prospect of order and stable government at the Restoration, and he showed no sympathy with the demands of the more extreme sectaries and the disturbances they caused. In apparently marked contrast with what has been regarded as the 'liberalism'

[1] There is another technical legal sense of the word sovereignty which I am also not referring to here, viz. the status of an independent, autonomous state in international law.

of his maturity, Locke's outlook in 1660 revealed itself as conservative. In the preface to the English tract that he wrote (but did not publish) on the powers of the civil magistrate[1] he declared that 'the supreme magistrate of every nation . . . must necessarily have an *absolute* and *arbitrary power* over all the indifferent actions of his people'. This was so 'whether the magistrate's crown drops down on his head immediately from *heaven* or be placed there by the *hands of his subjects*'. In the tract itself he explained that 'by magistrate I understand the supreme legislative power of any society, not considering the form of government or number of persons wherein it is placed'. Even if man were

naturally owner of an entire liberty, and so much master of himself as to own no subjection to any other but God alone (which is the freest condition we can fancy him in), it is yet the unalterable condition of society and government that every particular man must unavoidably part with this right to his liberty and entrust the magistrate with as full a power over all his actions as he himself hath. . . . Nor do men . . . enjoy any greater share of this freedom in a pure commonwealth . . . than in an absolute monarchy, the same arbitrary power being there in the assembly . . . as in a monarch, wherein each particular man hath no more power (bating the inconsiderable addition of his single vote) of himself to make new or dispute old laws than in a monarchy; all he can do (which is no more than kings allow petitioners) is to persuade the majority which is the monarch.[2]

These and other passages have led to the conclusion that in his early life Locke was echoing the ideas of Hobbes.[3]

[1] Locke wrote two tracts about this time, one in English, the other in Latin. See P. Abrams (ed.), *John Locke, Two Tracts on Government* (Cambridge, 1967). [2] Ibid., pp. 122-3, 125.
[3] It has even been maintained that Locke was really a Hobbist all his life: cf. L. Strauss, *Natural Right and History* (Chicago, 1953), and R. Cox, *Locke on Peace and War* (Oxford, 1960).

Locke may well have felt, indeed he can hardly have helped feeling, the influence of Hobbes, but the high value he placed on the blessings of law and order at the time of the Restoration may be sufficiently explained by his revulsion from what he called 'the stinging swarms of miseries that attend anarchy and rebellion', without assuming that his ideas were directly borrowed from Hobbes.[1] Be that as it may, there can be no doubt that Locke clearly understood the meaning of legislative sovereignty, and whether he got this from Hobbes, or from Filmer, who stated it as unmistakably as Hobbes, is immaterial. The question that concerns us now is whether he still retained his belief in the necessity of a sovereign authority when he came to write *Two Treatises of Government*. He was engaged then in refuting Filmer, and instead of laying his chief emphasis on the advantages of firmness and stability in government he was insisting rather on its responsibility, and its liability to be turned out if it failed to discharge its trust. It is true that he changed his phraseology, and no longer described the legislative power as absolute and arbitrary. In fact he now declared that the legislative power 'is not nor possibly can be absolutely arbitrary over the lives and fortunes of the people'.[2] He reserved the word 'arbitrary' for power that contravened the law of nature, and avoided calling the legislature 'sovereign'. But he always insisted that it was 'supreme', and stated clearly that by the social compact every man surrenders his natural liberty and 'puts himself under an obligation . . . to submit to the determination of the majority, and to be concluded by it'.[3] The legislature was indeed under an

[1] P. Abrams, op. cit., p. 156. On the difficult question of the relation of Locke's thought to Hobbes's see also ibid., p. 75, and P. Laslett's Introduction to his edition of *Two Treatises of Government* (Cambridge, 1960), pp. 21, 67 ff.

[2] *Second Treatise*, § 135.   [3] § 97.

obligation to serve 'the public good', and the law of nature applied 'as an eternal rule to all men, legislators as well as others',[1] so that a government which violated these conditions might be overthrown by a popular revolt; but in effect, while it lasted, it was sovereign, in the sense that there was no constitutional machinery to limit it.[2] On this question, in fact, Locke's views remained substantially unchanged, for the powers he ascribed to the magistrate in his tract of 1660 extended only over 'indifferent things', by which he meant things on which natural law, or the law of God, laid down no rule. And while he insisted in 1660 on the need for firm government, he at the same time professed himself a lover of liberty, for he believed, then and afterwards, that the one could not be had without the other.

In the course of the seventeenth century the meaning and implications of legislative sovereignty came to be generally understood, but for many years its acceptance was checked by the persistence of the notion of fundamental law, which, it was widely believed, was a positive limit to the capacity of legislation.[3] This idea, fostered especially by upholders of the common law, was often associated with the idea of an ancient constitution, much canvassed by Whig historians, according to whom parliament, including the House of Commons, and the liberties it was supposed to maintain, had existed since Anglo-Saxon times, and the Norman Conquest had not really been a conquest at all. Filmer, and the Tories who adopted his views, were as much concerned to refute this

[1] § 135.
[2] Cf. C. B. Macpherson, *The Political Theory of Possessive Individualism* (Oxford, 1962), pp. 258–60. But see also below, p. 125.
[3] I have discussed this question at length in my *Fundamental Law in English Constitutional History* (Oxford, revised impression, 1971) and will not repeat or attempt to summarize it here.

version of history as to insist on the divinity of the right of kings. Though belief in fundamental law declined in face of the unmistakable fact of legislative sovereignty, the Whig version of English constitutional history long persisted, one of its champions being Locke's friend James Tyrrell; but Locke himself rested his opposition to royal absolutism not so much on history, or the obsolescent idea of fundamental law, as on natural law and reason. As far as the separation of powers is concerned, he thought it advisable that the legislative and executive should be kept apart, but there was no suggestion that either of them should act as a positive check or limit to the power of the other. Thus while Montesquieu may have owed some of his ideas and phraseology to Locke, in this respect there was a clear difference between them. Montesquieu's principle implied a denial of sovereignty, whereas Locke's was consistent with the sovereignty of the king in parliament.

The sovereignty of the king in parliament, of course, was no indivisible or undivided power, like the sovereignty of a Hobbesian monarch, but one shared between different bodies, who would have to co-operate harmoniously for it to be exercised successfully.[1] Strictly speaking, the legal sovereign today is still the king in parliament, just as much as in the seventeenth century, so that in a formal sense the legal sovereign today is no less divided than it was then. But then the king had a real share of power, whereas today the royal assent is only a form. It may be objected that parliament consists of two houses, and that though the House of Lords has now been shorn of most of its power, I am not keeping strictly to the legal sense of the term if by the sovereignty of parliament I really mean the sovereignty of the House of Commons. It is, indeed,

[1] Filmer, in fact, had denounced a 'mixed monarchy' as equivalent to anarchy, because its component parts quarrelled instead of co-operating.

obvious that legal sovereignty is not an ultimate stopping-point, but leads on to consideration of the 'political sovereignty' that lies behind it, whether this be the power of the government, with which rests the effective initiative in legislation, or 'the sovereignty of the people', on whom the choice of a government depends. We may perhaps say that political sovereignty is what Locke attributed to the people, in whom 'there remains still . . . a supreme power to remove or alter the legislative when they find the legislative act contrary to the trust reposed in them'; but this supremacy of the people is 'not as considered under any form of government, because the power of the people can never take place till the government be dissolved'.[1] Locke has been blamed for not providing proper constitutional machinery, as in a modern democratic state, by which the people could regularly exercise their political sovereignty, instead of relying on the hazardous and clumsy remedy of a revolution when their patience had been exhausted.[2] But Locke was not a modern democrat. He would not have approved of a popular franchise, and was satisfied, like his fellow Whigs, with what they venerated as the traditional constitution.

While the legislature was to be supreme, it was to exercise its power subject to the law of nature, and Locke laid down the specific conditions he thought necessary to secure this. In the first place, the legislature is 'sacred and unalterable in the hands where the community have once placed it'.[3] Further, 'it is not nor possibly can be absolutely arbitrary over the lives and fortunes of the people', nor can it 'assume to itself a power to rule by extemporary arbitrary decrees, but is bound to dispense justice, and decide the rights of the subject, by promulgated standing laws,

---

[1] *Second Treatise*, §§ 149, 150.   [2] See above, pp. 45, 46.
[3] *Second Treatise*, § 143.

and known authorized judges';[1] and these laws are to be equal for all classes and 'designed for no other end . . . but the good of the people'.[2] It cannot 'take from any man any part of his property without his own consent',[3] and, lastly, 'being but a delegated power from the people', it 'cannot transfer the power of making laws to any other hands'.[4] It is 'only a fiduciary power to act for certain ends',[5] namely the promotion of 'the public good' in accordance with the 'fundamental law of nature', which enjoins 'the preservation of mankind'.[6] For this reason 'the community perpetually retains a supreme power of saving themselves from the attempts and designs of anybody . . . so foolish and wicked as to lay and carry on designs against the liberties and properties of the subject.'[7]

The reason Locke gives for these limitations to the power of the legislature is that it is 'but the joint power of every member of the society given up to that person, or assembly, which is legislator'. In the state of nature 'nobody has an absolute arbitrary power over himself, or over any other, to destroy his own life, or take away the life and property of another', and 'nobody can transfer to another more power than he has in himself'.[8] This follows from Locke's theory of the origin of the state in a compact of individuals; but even if we dismiss all this as a mere product of the philosophical imagination, the resultant limitation of the power of the government was no figment, but a rationalization of accepted constitutional practice.

Locke's political theory has been described as an attack not only on the sovereignty of *Leviathan* but on the very

---

[1] *Second Treatise*, §§ 135, 136.   [2] § 142.
[3] § 138. As we have seen, however (cf. p. 76, above), it can tax by majority-vote.
[4] § 141.   [5] § 149.   [6] § 135.
[7] § 149.   [8] § 135.

idea of sovereignty.[1] Dr. Figgis complained that while Locke realized that the legislature is supreme, he fenced it about with various limitations, and, instead of saying that the transgression of these limits is inexpedient or iniquitous, tried to prove that it would be illegal. The notion of legal omnipotence was abhorrent to him, and in consequence he was 'guilty of a confusion between law natural and law positive from which the extremest and most reactionary royalist would have been free'.[2] On the contrary, as it seems to me, Locke was quite well aware of the difference between natural and positive law, though it is true that his point of view was not that of the twentieth century, and that he regarded natural law, which he equated with the will of God, as something more than a mere moral obligation. Locke, like Bodin, thought of the government as bound by the obligation of natural law—with a duty, that is, to rule for the public good, and with a responsibility to the community (which he expressed in terms of trusteeship) for framing its policy accordingly. He did not, however, conceive of the government as limited by positive law, and this is where his theory clearly differs from that which inspired the framers of the American constitution. With them the rigid separation of powers and the written constitution itself were positive guarantees that no branch of the government should exceed its assigned limits or be superior to any other branch.

It is true that Locke used the expression 'fundamental law', even 'fundamental positive law', but by this he meant to emphasize the binding force of the original act of the people when they set up a legislature. He did not

---

[1] J. N. Figgis, *The Divine Right of Kings*, p. 242; C. E. Vaughan, *Studies in the History of Political Philosophy before and after Rousseau*, i. 134.
[2] Figgis, loc. cit.

assert, as some lawyers had asserted earlier in the century, that the courts could decline to enforce an act of parliament. On the contrary, while the government lasts, he recognizes not only that the legislature is supreme, but also that there is no constitutional or legal machinery for overriding it. Such action can only be extra-constitutional, and if it abuses its trust, the only remedy is revolution. Those who preached divine right and non-resistance admitted no such right in the people to 'appeal to Heaven'; Locke, on the other hand, was saying in effect that there were circumstances in which revolt was morally justifiable. Enlightened modern opinion would agree with him.

Did this amount to a denial of the very idea of sovereignty? In a strict sense I think we must agree that it did. If a legislature is truly and fully sovereign, this is commonly taken to mean not only that the validity of its enactments is unchallengeable, but also that it can change the constitution itself by ordinary legislative process. This Locke's legislature certainly cannot do; the constitution as settled at the original compact is to remain apparently fixed for ever.[1] Apart from this point, Locke's view of the

---

[1] One consequence of this restriction is that the legislature itself is incapable of disfranchising decayed boroughs and creating new constituencies. Locke recognizes 'to what gross absurdities the following of custom when reason has left it may lead, when we see the bare name of a town, of which there remains not so much as the ruins, . . . sends as many representatives to the grand assembly of law-makers as a whole county numerous in people'; but the only remedy he can offer is that the executive, following the maxim *salus populi suprema lex*, should undertake where necessary a redistribution of seats. In so doing, he thinks, 'it cannot be judged to have set up a new legislative, but to have restored the old and true one' (§§ 157, 158). It is easy to scoff at the notion that the king had, but parliament had not, a right to disfranchise Old Sarum (Sir James Stephen, *Horae Sabbaticae*, 2nd series, ix. 155), but apart from the logical necessity of this in Locke's system, it was, in fact, in accordance with historical precedent, for new borough constituencies had always been created by royal writ. Nevertheless, the recent example of Newark in Charles II's reign had been challenged.

legislature as supreme, yet under the restraint of natural law, is substantially the same as that expressed in the reign of Elizabeth I by Peter Wentworth. Sir John Neale paraphrases it thus: 'Parliament was not sovereign, according to modern Austinian ideas. It had a sphere of power within which it was "absolute", in the sense that there was no superior authority to overrule it, but within that sphere it operated subject to the fundamental principles of God's law and natural law—principles, that is to say, of justice and equity.[1]

Ideas like these were constantly repeated during the following century, and were evidently shared by Locke. In this context he avoided the word 'sovereignty', perhaps because of its association with Leviathan and arbitrary power, which he clearly wished to rule out.[2] He substituted the words 'supreme power', and his use of this term may seem confused at first sight, for he applied it to the legislature, and to the 'single person', and to the people themselves; but his meaning is really plain enough, and in terms of sovereignty may be interpreted thus. The legislature, in the first place, though not fully sovereign in the modern sense, occupies a position corresponding to that of the legal sovereign. The king is not technically sovereign at all, but as a title he is commonly called the sovereign. This is really a survival from the older medieval sense of the word, before it came to acquire a technical meaning, and Locke only says that when he is head of the executive and also shares in the legislative the 'single person in a very tolerable sense may . . . be called supreme'. The people, to whom the legislature is responsible, is 'political sovereign', but this

[1] J. E. Neale, *Elizabeth I and her Parliaments, 1584–1601* (1957), p. 262.

[2] The word occurs in a number of places, in both of the *Two Treatises* (e.g. i, §§ 129, 131, 133; ii, §§ 4, 115), generally meaning absolute power. In § 108, the 'kings' of the American Indians are said to 'have but a very moderate sovereignty'.

sovereignty he regards as normally in abeyance, and it only takes effect when the government has been dissolved. Locke thus avoids the confusion in which Rousseau became involved, when in the attempt to make the political and the legal sovereign correspond, he ascribed sovereignty to the general will and thought it could only be ascertained in small communities. Locke makes a passing reference to democratic government as a theoretical possibility,[1] but he evidently did not think it worth serious consideration. The power of the people, in his system, is exercised at the foundation of the state, but after that it remains dormant unless a revolution becomes necessary, for the established government is sacrosanct so long as it fulfils its trust. Locke accepted, in fact, the political outlook normal in his day, but his concept of trusteeship served to reinforce the notion that governments are not arbitrary and irresponsible organs of power, but have a responsibility to promote the public welfare.

Locke's constitution, and the structure of society in his age, would obviously be unsatisfactory today, and in the two centuries and more that have elapsed since the Revolution we have widened the franchise and developed the system of cabinet government as a means of making that responsibility more effective. One result of this has been that whereas in his day executive and legislature were largely (though not rigidly) distinct, and, often deliberately, controlled and checked each other, our modern constitution has come to lose some of the old checks which used to prevent the possibility of arbitrary government. In the seventeenth century it seemed to many that the main danger to be guarded against came from the pretentions of monarchy and its supporters. It was to check these that parliamentarians and common-lawyers stressed

[1] *Second Treatise,* § 132.

their theories of fundamental law, mixed government, and the separation of powers. The upshot was the establishment of the supremacy of parliament over the king, and the capture by parliament, through the machinery of the cabinet, of the royal power, now exercised by ministers responsible to parliament. It was in these circumstances that the sovereignty of parliament was accepted and welcomed as an organ of liberty, whereas the sovereignty of the king would have been condemned as tyrannical. In practice, eighteenth-century parliaments were not only absurdly unrepresentative but at times extremely irresponsible and high-handed in their actions, and the question was raised (by the Americans, for example, and by John Wilkes; just as in the previous century it had been raised by opponents of the Rump), whether the arbitrary power of a parliament was necessarily to be preferred to the arbitrary power of a king. In the nineteenth century the need to answer this question was postponed for a time by the movement for parliamentary reform, but nowadays, when the sovereignty of parliament means in effect the sovereignty of a majority in the House of Commons, and this in turn is under the direction of a party cabinet, it may be time to think again.

The legal doctrine of parliamentary omnipotence could never have persisted, Professor McIlwain suggests, if its edge had not been blunted by conventions, and he believes that when these conventions lose their effectiveness there will be a demand for law, and the conventions will either be turned into law, or be abandoned altogether. So it was that in the eighteenth century the Americans thought it necessary to embody the doctrine of the separation of powers in a written constitution; and he notices that in more recent times it has once more been in imperial matters that law has been substituted for convention, by the enactment in 1931 of the Statute of Westminster. Professor McIlwain calls the separation of powers a figment of the imagination of eighteenth-century doctrinaires, who found it in our earlier history only because of their ignorance. It was indeed a 'false theory of the English state',[1] for in the Middle Ages, while there was a very definite doctrine of the limitation of powers, there was no doctrine of their separation. To limit government, he continues, is not necessarily to weaken it, and in the light of experience of the working of the American constitution he condemns any artificial system of checks and balances as unknown before the eighteenth century, almost untried before the nineteenth, and disastrous wherever tried since. This, surely, goes too far, for the idea of the separation of powers was known in England in the seventeenth century, and the embodiment of a system of checks and balances in a written constitution was tried—not very successfully, it must be admitted—during the Protectorate of Oliver Cromwell. Professor McIlwain, however, returns to the old distinction between *gubernaculum* and *jurisdictio*, and sees in law the best safeguard against arbitrary will. What is needed therefore, he thinks, is 'an honest, able, learned, independent judiciary'.[2]

England, he remarks, is probably the most constitutional of modern nations, not because its constitution is embodied in any formal document, but because its form of government preserves an inheritance of free institutions, based on precedent and convention as well as written law. This inheritance can be traced back to the Middle Ages, when Bracton distinguished between *gubernaculum* (the government of the realm, in the sense of its effective

[1] Cf. above, pp. 104, 113.
[2] C. H. McIlwain, *Constitutionalism Ancient and Modern* (Ithaca, N.Y., 1940), pp. 20, 144–6.

administration, which was in the king's hands and in which he could not be questioned) and *jurisdictio*, which must be according to law or custom, and which was thus the guarantee of private rights and liberties. This distinction was still the key to the English constitution at the end of the sixteenth century: private right was determinable only by law, under the control of the courts and parliament, while matters of state were in the sphere of the royal prerogative, which was absolute and indisputable. The delicate balance between these two broke down, however, in the seventeenth century, when the king and his supporters aimed at the subordination of *jurisdictio* to *gubernaculum*, while the parliamentarians and common lawyers sought to extend their idea of fundamental law into a barrier against absolute power in every sphere.[2]

Nowadays the old idea of fundamental law as a limit to the sovereignty of parliament has long been extinct in England, and since the courts therefore cannot annul an act of parliament on the grounds of its repugnancy to fundamental law, the judiciary is no longer in a position to be a safeguard against the danger of a tyranny of the majority. Hitherto we have escaped this danger because (and this, I think, is one of the main reasons why parliamentary government has flourished and survived in this country, whereas in many other countries it has either perished or never taken root) party rivalry has not cut so deep as to undermine what, for lack of a better phrase, I can only call the fundamental principles of the constitution.[2] These, admittedly, are no longer legal fundamentals. There is no legal distinction in England between public and private law, between the law affecting a vital element of the constitution and the law regulating the most trivial

[1] C. H. McIlwain, op. cit., pp. 17, 79 ff., 114.
[2] Cf. above, p. 59.

domestic affairs. One way of putting this is to say, with de Tocqueville, that the English constitution does not exist. While both parties tacitly agreed to respect these principles, there was no immediate risk in their being at the mercy of a legally sovereign parliament under the political control of a party cabinet. Though the House of Lords before 1911 often used its powers foolishly, and had itself largely to blame for their curtailment in the Parliament Act, it was nevertheless a safeguard against the irresponsible exercise of power by a party temporarily controlling a majority in the House of Commons. Since then the powers of the House of Lords have been still further curtailed, and some have doubted whether it is any longer safe, without a written constitution, to put sovereignty, or in other words the opportunity to wield arbitrary power, into the hands of a party majority in a single chamber.

These circumstances led Charles Morgan to urge[1] that we should reconsider, in the light of Montesquieu's doctrine, the old arguments in favour of legal limitations to arbitrary rule. Such a suggestion, however, seems to me wholly academic, and I cannot conceive that our modern parliamentary democracy would agree to accept the rigid constitutional checks of the American type of government.[2] This originated as much from the practical need to satisfy the claims of the states, which necessitated a federal constitution, as from the political theories of Locke or Montesquieu. The dangers Morgan had in mind, however, are neither academic nor imaginary, and more recently we have heard doubts expressed whether the

[1] In the Zaharoff Lecture for 1948, at Oxford.

[2] In a revised version of his lecture, published in *Liberties of the Mind* (1951), pp. 57–80, Morgan stressed the need for a reformed Second Chamber.

parliamentary system itself still enjoys the confidence of the public, and suggestions that nothing short of direct (i.e. revolutionary) action can achieve the desired results. It is to be hoped that, though Morgan's demand for law be unheard, party majorities, and the more impatient of their supporters, may nevertheless discipline themselves to respect, instead of abandoning, the principles of the constitution. Otherwise, although we may profess to eschew totalitarianism, we may, when it is too late, have cause to regret the disappearance of the safeguards against arbitrary power which our ancestors regarded as one of their chief blessings.

VI

LOCKE AND THE
ENGLISH REVOLUTION

UNTIL a few years ago there seemed to be nothing specially controversial or hard to interpret about the historical significance of Locke's political theory. In general terms he was essentially the Whig philosopher: more particularly his name was associated with the so-called Glorious Revolution of 1688. There was some disagreement about the exact nature of this association, but he was commonly described as the apologist for the Revolution, and this was often understood to mean that his purpose in writing his *Two Treatises of Government* was to 'justify' the Revolution and the Whig principles of government—the original contract and limited monarchy—which thereby triumphed over the Tory doctrines of non-resistance and the divine right of kings. But even before Mr. Peter Laslett published the results of his masterly investigation of the date of composition of the *Two Treatises*, to which we shall come presently, there were some versions of Locke's achievement that were obviously untenable. It could not be true, in the first place, that Locke supplied the arguments used by the Whig politicians in the Convention. Apart from the fact that these arguments had been the familiar stock-in-trade of the writers of political tracts and pamphlets for a generation and more before the Revolution, Locke's *Treatises* were not published until the Revolution was over,[1] and

[1] 1690 is the date on the title-page of the first edition. It was licensed for printing on 23 August 1689, and copies were for sale in November of that year.

at the time of the Revolution he was still in exile in Holland. He seems to have been concerned, in a minor capacity, with the preparation of the plans for William of Orange's expedition to England, but there is no reason to suppose that he was in touch with the politicians in England, or that they needed him to supply them with ideas. It is clear, then, that even if Locke were the philosopher of the Revolution, this could not mean that he inspired it. Nor could it mean simply that the Revolution inspired him, because there is plenty of evidence, in his journals and note-books, that he had been a student of politics, as of other branches of philosophy, for years, and that he had already reached his main conclusions long before he came to write the *Treatises*.

Another suggestion seems to be that Locke took the arguments used by the revolutionary politicians, cast them into a philosophical shape, and worked them up into a connected treatise, which was subsequently accepted as a kind of Whig political gospel. But he had no need to go to the politicians for his arguments, for, like the politicians themselves, he could have found them all, and others besides, in the mass of controversial publications which poured from the press during the political crises of the seventeenth century. He had many of these works in his library, and his note-books show that he continually reflected and commented on the subjects of his reading. Secondly, some of his arguments differed from the arguments actually used by the revolutionary politicians. One of the most famous of these was the 'original contract between king and people', which James II was accused of breaking; and because there is a contract or compact in Locke's system, it has sometimes been assumed that Locke's contract was this celebrated commonplace of the Whig politicians. But Locke's contract is not a 'contract of government' between king and people, but an agreement between individuals to form a civil society and 'submit to the determination of the majority'. The establishment of the organs of government is subsequent to this, and does not take the form of a contract; instead, the people place 'a fiduciary power' in the hands of the government, which can be removed if it acts 'contrary to the trust reposed in it'. More recent writers have recognized this characteristic doctrine of Locke's,[1] but sometimes still with a tendency to regard it as equivalent, in spirit if not in letter, to a contract.[2] The notion of the political trust had long been widely current in seventeenth-century England, and, together with the contract of government, was freely used at the time of the Revolution;[3] but it was the contract, and not the trust-concept, which actually found a place in the famous resolution of the Convention Parliament.

Considerations like these necessitated some modification of the traditional interpretation of Locke. His work, it was suggested, was not primarily or in intention an apologia for the Revolution of 1688, though it was subsequently recognized and accepted as such. The *First Treatise*, admittedly, was a controversial work in refutation of Filmer, but this had only a transient interest in its own day and could now be ignored. The *Second Treatise*, on the

[1] e.g. C. E. Vaughan, in *Studies in the History of Political Philosophy Before and After Rousseau* (Manchester, 1925), i. 145; E. Barker, correcting O. Gierke in *Natural Law and the Theory of Society* (Cambridge, 1934), ii. 299, and in the Introduction to his *Social Contract* (Oxford, 1947), p. xxvi.

[2] Thus C. E. Vaughan (loc. cit.) argued that a trust can be revoked by the trustor whenever he likes, but the trust conferred on the government by the people can only be revoked when broken by the trustee. Therefore, he maintained, it approaches the notion of contract. A contract, however, while it implies obligations, implies also that both parties have rights. The idea of trust suited Locke better, because it placed the government in a more definitely disadvantageous position.

[3] See p. 174, below.

other hand, was primarily a philosophical work, offering solutions of general problems such as the nature of political obligation and the relationship between the individual and the state.[1] This was not to deny that it takes its place in the history of political philosophy, and is controversial to the extent that it naturally gives prominence to topics which occupied the forefront of attention at the time. So much, however, is true of even the most academic philosophical works, and Locke's political theory was to be judged, therefore, by its success or failure as an exercise of intellectual speculation. Scrutinized from this point of view, it was easy to show that Locke is full of illogical flaws and inconsistencies, and that his conception of civil society as an association formed for limited purposes by a contract of individuals involves a wholly inadequate estimate of the part to be played by the state in human life. Moreover, the critic who adopted this interpretation of Locke was apt to blame him when he met, as he could not help meeting, with passages which, while purporting to have a general application, had an obvious reference to the conditions of his own time.[2] Poor Locke! He is censured on the one hand because his state of nature is an abstraction peopled with imaginary beings, and on the other because the conditions he describes are recognizably those of contemporary England.

The truth is, surely, that although neither of these interpretations will stand up by itself, neither is wholly

[1] This is the line taken by Mr. Willmoore Kendall, op. cit., p. 67. Cf. also G. R. Driver in *Social and Political Ideas of Some English Thinkers of the Augustan Age* (ed. Hearnshaw, 1928), p. 78, and Ch. Bastide, *John Locke, ses théories politiques et leur influence en Angleterre* (Paris, 1906), p. 262.

[2] Thus Vaughan remarks that Locke's law of nature purports to be 'plain and intelligible to every rational creature', but it turns out to be little more than 'a transcript of the usages which he found established in his own country', blended with 'considerations of pure equity: though of equity determined . . . by the most humane standards of the author's own day and country' (op. cit., p. 181).

erroneous. The original composition of the *Two Treatises* was not inspired by the Revolution, but this does not mean that it was a purely abstract study entirely unconnected with events. Nor was its publication just after the Revolution simply a coincidence. In the Preface Locke stated explicitly that he hoped 'to establish the throne of our great restorer, our present King William; to make good his title in the consent of the people, . . . and to justify to the world the people of England, whose love of their just and natural rights, with their resolution to preserve them, saved the nation when it was on the very brink of slavery and ruin'. When Locke published his work he obviously intended to 'justify' the proceedings of the Revolution and the form of government that emerged from them, though not necessarily all the arguments used by the Whig politicians. Two more editions of the book were published in Locke's lifetime, the second edition in 1694, the third in 1698, and I do not think we can be mistaken in seeing in it his interpretation of the contemporary constitution, and the reasons why he approved of it. But it was also more than a *pièce d'occasion*, and has survived as one of the classics of political thought, whereas nearly all the other innumerable publications of the time have been forgotten. *Two Treatises of Government* was published anonymously, and though Locke's authorship became widely suspected, and known to a few friends, he persisted in doing his utmost to conceal his connexion with the work, and it was not until after his death that editions were published with his name on the title-page. Various reasons have been suggested for this attitude: Locke's cautious temperament (Algernon Sidney had been executed for treason largely on account of his writings), or his uncomfortable awareness that the *Two Treatises* and the *Essay concerning Human Understanding* were fundamentally inconsistent. But though

Locke was unwilling to be known as the author, in the eighteenth century the repute of the *Two Treatises* was undoubtedly enhanced by the fact that it came from the same pen as the celebrated *Essay*. Locke was not merely a political pamphleteer, but a professional philosopher. His political philosophy was admittedly not original, but the fruit of years of wide reading and reflection, and the materials out of which his system was built can be paralleled in the writings of numerous predecessors and contemporaries.[1] But if he 'justified' the constitutional principles of the Revolution Whigs, he did so not merely by urging their expediency in the circumstances, but by making them appear to be in accordance with the conclusions of pure reason. It was this appeal to the rational temper of his age, reinforced by his skill in expressing himself in a clear, unpretentious, and readable style, which accounted for his success then, and the remarkable influence he exercised over generations to come.

Besides his journals and commonplace books, Locke wrote a good deal in his earlier years, including two preliminary drafts of the *Essay concerning Human Understanding*,

---

[1] Cf. the article by A. H. Maclean in *Cambridge Historical Journal*, ix, no. 1 (1947), pp. 69–77, drawing attention to the close parallel between Locke's theories and those put forward by the Rev. George Lawson in *An Examination of the Political Part of Mr. Hobbes his Leviathan* (1657), and *Politica Sacra et Civilis* (1660). But we should be cautious in concluding that Lawson was the, or a, source of Locke's ideas. Nothing could stand in greater contrast than the style and manner of Lawson and Locke. Locke wrote in easy, flowing, if sometimes rather long-winded sentences, while Lawson set out his arguments in a repellently schematic form. Professor C. H. McIlwain pointed out the similarity between Locke's *Treatise* and Philip Hunton's *Treatise of Monarchy* (first published in 1643 and reprinted in 1689), in *Politica*, i (1934–5), pp. 243–73. Locke's characteristic arguments, in fact, had long been commonplaces of political theory, but the conclusion to be drawn from this is not necessarily that he deliberately, or even unconsciously, plagiarized this author or that. They were part of the usual mental furniture of every 'liberal' thinker of his age.

and a number of short treatises, notes, and memoranda on a variety of philosophical and political topics, including that of toleration. Nothing of his had been published,[1] however, before 1689, when his *Epistola de Tolerantia* appeared anonymously in Holland, and was translated into English in the same year, to be followed by the *Two Treatises of Government* and the *Essay*. The completion of these works seems to have been the fruit of his exile in Holland, where he lived from 1683 to 1689. For some time before this he had been in the service of Lord Shaftesbury, and had thus been in close contact with one of the headquarters of political activity in England during the crisis over the Exclusion Bill. This crisis, like the Revolution a few years later, and the critical years of the Civil War and the Interregnum a generation earlier, was the occasion for a considerable output of controversial tracts and pamphlets. Among them, in 1679, was a reissue of a collection of Filmer's political tracts, followed next year by his major work, *Patriarcha*,[2] and the appearance of these works in support of the Tory side immediately stimulated a number of writers to reply to them. One of these was James Tyrrell, whose *Patriarcha Non Monarcha* appeared in 1681.[3] Locke stayed at Tyrrell's house at Oakley, near Brill, in Buckinghamshire, about this time, and collaborated with him in a work defending nonconformity and toleration against the attacks of Edward Stillingfleet, later Bishop of Worcester.[4] It is conceivable, though improbable, that he also had a

---

[1] Except for a few youthful poems.

[2] Although not published until 1680, this had been written before the Civil War, and was, in fact, Filmer's earliest work. Filmer died in 1653.

[3] Another was Algernon Sidney, whose *Discourses concerning Government* were written in 1681, but not published till 1698, after his death.

[4] The manuscript of this work, extracts from which were printed by Lord King in his *Life of John Locke* (Bohn's edn., 1858, p. 346) is in the Lovelace Collection, now in the Bodleian Library. See below, pp. 217–18.

hand in *Patriarcha Non Monarcha*. Besides this, Locke himself was impelled to try his own hand at an answer to
Filmer, but before he had published it, the Revolution
took place. This meant a dramatic change in his personal fortunes, and he returned to England in the same
ship as the Princess Mary. The Revolution, and the
constitutional settlement that followed it, seemed to him a
triumphant vindication of the principles he had always
upheld, and it appears that he thereupon revised the
plan of his projected book, and decided to cut short his
refutation of Filmer, and conclude with a constructive
statement of his theory of government in the light of the
recent revolution.

This, at any rate, seems a likely explanation of the somewhat cryptic opening sentences of the Preface to the *Two
Treatises of Government*, in which the reader is informed
that the book in his hands is 'the beginning and end of a
discourse concerning government', but that "tis not worth
while to tell' him 'what fate has otherwise disposed of the
papers that should have filled up the middle, and were
more than all the rest'. We may presume that 'the beginning' comprises the attack on Filmer in the *First Treatise*,
and that by 'the end' is meant the whole or part of what
we now know as the *Second Treatise*. The missing passages
(whether they were deliberately suppressed by Locke, or
were lost or destroyed by accident is not known) were
presumably concerned with a further and more detailed
examination of Filmer, for in a later sentence in the Preface Locke remarks that he has 'neither the time nor the
inclination to repeat my pains and fill up the wanting part
of my answer by tracing Sir Robert again through all the
windings and obscurities . . . of his wonderful system'. This
points to a change of mind in Locke, and he may well have
felt that, since the Revolution had decided the issue of

divine right, the lengthy and elaborate discourse he had originally planned against Filmer was no longer needed. Instead, he would make a general philosophical discussion of the origins and nature of the state lead up to a justification of the Revolution, and so present the constitutional settlement as the logical outcome of rational principles of government. So we have *An Essay concerning the True Original, Extent and End of Civil Government*, which is commonly known as the *Second Treatise*.

This does not mean, however, as has been thought, that Locke wrote the whole *Second Treatise* in the few months between his return to England in February 1689 and the application for a licence to print in early August. Apart from other considerations, such haste would be quite out of keeping with what we know of Locke's character and methods of composition. His biographer Fox Bourne suggested that Locke wrote the *First Treatise* in 1681 or 1682, and had substantially completed the *Second Treatise* before the end of his exile in Holland. This is more likely than the idea that he wrote the whole *Second Treatise* in 1689, in substitution for the lost or suppressed conclusion of the *First Treatise*, but in fact internal evidence points to the *Second Treatise*, or at any rate parts of it, having been written some years earlier than this. For instance, in two places[1] James I was referred to in the first edition simply as King James, although in 1689 readers might have taken this to mean James II. The most likely explanation is that the passages in which these references occur were written before 1685, and overlooked when the book first went to press. One of them was corrected in the second edition, the other in the third. This point seems not to have been noticed until Mr. Laslett drew attention to it, and to a number of other allusions which fit the circumstances of the Exclu-

[1] In §§ 133 and 200.

sion crisis in Charles II's reign rather than the events of James II's. Not only so, but as the result of a careful and exact examination of such points as the dates (known from Locke's manuscript diaries and book-lists) when Locke acquired certain editions of the works of Filmer and other writers quoted or referred to in his text, Laslett has argued that the *Two Treatises* must have been completed between 1679 and 1681, or 1683 at the latest.[1] This conclusion regarding the date of composition of Locke's work is now generally accepted.

Locke may have gone on working over and revising his book while he was in Holland, and after the Revolution he evidently made further alterations, adding some passages where necessary in order to adapt it to the new circumstances of its publication. Another point of interest to which Laslett has drawn attention is that in the Preface Locke refers not to 'two treatises' but 'a discourse' on government, and he concludes that originally it was not divided into two parts. He points out that a number of topics are broached in what is now the *First Treatise*, but a full discussion of them is postponed to the *Second Treatise*, and he believes that in its original form the 'discourse' began with the substance of what is now the *Second Treatise*, in defence of the traditional English constitution, apparently threatened by Charles II; then, when *Patriarcha* was published in 1680, Locke decided that he must add a detailed refutation of Filmer. After the Revolution he abbreviated the latter and made it stand at the beginning of the published work. This perhaps is more conjectural, but Mr. Laslett is clearly right in maintaining that the

[1] See his article, 'The English Revolution and Locke's "Two Treatises of Government" ', in *Cambridge Historical Journal*, xii, no. 1 (1956), pp. 40–55, and J. Locke, *Two Treatises of Government* (ed. P. Laslett, Cambridge, 1960), pp. 45–66.

whole work, and not only the *First Treatise*, was designed as a reply to Filmer. This is evident not only in such references as that to Filmer's idea of freedom in § 22, but in the chapters on property, on paternal power, on conquest, and elsewhere in the *Second Treatise*. Laslett further argues that Locke's original purpose was to justify, not a revolution that had already happened, but one that was being planned: that he was in fact far more deeply committed to Shaftesbury's plots against Charles II than his biographers have admitted, and that it was not without good cause that he was suspected of treason and fled to Holland. How far Locke was deliberately composing propaganda in support of Shaftesbury's schemes is debatable. Dr. de Beer disagrees with Mr. Laslett on this, and prefers to regard Locke's work as a speculative treatise in answer to a speculative treatise by Filmer.[1]

Another consequence of Mr. Laslett's drastic refutation of traditional notions about Locke is that we must revise, if not abandon, the idea that, while the *First Treatise* was an attack on Filmer, his real target in the *Second Treatise* was Hobbes. Many writers on the history of political theory, while recognizing Locke's system as a characteristic statement of the contractual, anti-absolutist school of thought, seem to have regarded his historical importance as consisting essentially in his being a kind of link between Hobbes and Rousseau. Why then, they were inclined to ask, did he waste so much time on Filmer, whose ridiculous doctrines he so easily demolished, and never mention Hobbes, who was a far more important and serious opponent? For, they assumed, Locke's account in his *Second Treatise* of the state of nature, and of the kind of government set up to replace it as a result of the social contract,

[1] E. S. de Beer, 'Locke and English Liberalism', in J. W. Yolton (ed.), *John Locke: Problems and Perspectives* (Cambridge, 1969), pp. 34–44.

is essentially a denial of Hobbes's doctrines. This criticism, however, is to look at Locke's historical position in a false perspective. To critics in the nineteenth or twentieth centuries Filmer may well have appeared ridiculous (though recent years have seen him partly rehabilitated)[1] and Hobbes a far more significant figure in the history of political thought. In Locke's time, however, the relative importance of Filmer and Hobbes would have seemed very different. Hobbes's works had had a bad reception on all sides. Supporters and opponents of the monarchy alike repudiated his views, and he was accused of being immoral and an atheist. Clarendon denounced him in a work published in 1670;[2] and though Hobbes had a further shot to fire in later life,[3] by the end of Charles II's reign the excitement aroused by his works had largely subsided, and it was not until the time of Bentham, a hundred years later, that the significance of his theory of sovereignty began to be appreciated. This is not to deny that the system of government Locke advocated is an implicit repudiation of Hobbes, or that he himself recognized Hobbes's significance, and in places deliberately attacked him.[4] But

[1] Cf., for example, S. P. Lamprecht, *The Moral and Political Philosophy of John Locke* (New York, 1918), pp. 41 ff., and J. W. Allen in *Social and Political Ideas of Some English Thinkers of the Augustan Age* (ed. Hearnshaw, 1928), pp. 27 ff. And since then Mr. Laslett has edited Filmer for Messrs. Blackwell's Political Texts.

[2] *A Brief View and Survey of the Dangerous and Pernicious Errors to Church and State in Mr. Hobbes's Book entitled Leviathan.*

[3] *Behemoth*, published in 1679.

[4] An obvious place is in § 93, where he alludes scornfully to the notion that 'when men quitting the state of nature entered into society, they agreed that all of them but one should be under the restraint of laws, but that he should retain all the liberty of the state of nature, increased with power, and made licentious by impunity. This is to think that men are so foolish that they take care to avoid what mischief may be done them by polecats or foxes, but are content, nay, think it safety, to be devoured by lions.'

Filmer's doctrine was the recognized, one might almost say the official, creed of the Court and Tory party, and the issue at stake in the crisis over the Exclusion Bill was still to be decided at the Revolution.

If we examine the later chapters of Locke's *Second Treatise* in the light of this general interpretation, we shall find an integral connexion with contemporary history. The chapters in which he discusses the powers of government are in effect a description of the régime approved of in current Whig political thought. Like the rest of his theory, Locke made these appear to be the logical conclusion of ordinary common sense, but in fact they embody his observation of the traditional assumptions of the English constitution. Locke had had practical acquaintance with its operation, for he had been closely associated with Shaftesbury, and for a year or two had held political office under him. As I discuss the mechanism of Locke's system of government in a separate study, I will leave this subject here, and pass on to the last chapter of the *Second Treatise*, 'Of the Dissolution of Government'. The chapter opens by insisting that the dissolution of government must be distinguished from the dissolution of society itself, and this looks like an allusion to Hobbes, according to whom men would revert to the chaos of the state of nature immediately the restraining hand of the sovereign was removed. Locke, on the other hand, had been careful to keep the establishment of government separate from the compact by which men consented to form a society,[1] and his state of nature, as we have seen, was not chaotic but itself a

---

[1] In this Locke followed the usual line of contractarian theory, except that he made the establishment of government a trust instead of a second contract such as is found in Pufendorf and other writers of that school. Speakers in the Convention similarly argued that James II's action had dissolved the government, without implying that this involved a return to the state of nature.

social kind of existence. 'The usual and almost only way', he thinks, by which a society itself can be dissolved is by foreign conquest, which has often in the course of history cut societies in pieces, 'separating the subdued or scattered multitude from the protection of and dependence on that society which ought to have preserved them from violence'.[1]

If a society is thus destroyed, needless to say its government perishes with it, but besides this there are also ways in which 'governments are dissolved from within', and the first of these is 'when the legislative is altered'. It is hard to know, Locke blandly remarks, at whose door to lay the blame for this 'without knowing the form of government in which it happens. Let us suppose, then, the legislative placed in the concurrence of three distinct persons.' And so, in the thin disguise of an example 'supposed' in order to illustrate a general principle, we are invited to contemplate the contemporary English constitution:

'1. A single hereditary person having the constant supreme executive power, and with it the power of convoking and dissolving the other two within certain periods of time.

2. An assembly of hereditary nobility.

3. An assembly of representatives chosen *pro tempore* by the people.'[2]

Locke then proceeds to enumerate various methods in which the legislative may be 'altered'. First, the 'single person or prince' may 'set up his own arbitrary will in place of the laws which are the will of the society'; secondly, he may 'hinder the legislative from assembling in its due time, or from acting freely, pursuant to those ends for which it was constituted'. Thirdly, 'by the arbitrary power of the prince the electors or ways of election'

---

[1] *Second Treatise*, § 211.   [2] § 213.

may be altered, and this also amounts to an alteration of the legislative.[1] All this unmistakably refers, if in general terms, to recent English history, and so, too, does the fourth method, 'the delivery . . . of the people into the subjection of a foreign power'.[2] The Whigs blamed Charles II's foreign policy for its apparent subservience to Louis XIV; also, one of the chief counts against James II had been that he aimed to subject the country to the papacy. Locke adds another way in which governments are dissolved, and that is when either legislative or prince act contrary to their trust. This the legislative does if 'they endeavour to invade the property of the subject, and to make themselves or any part of the community masters or arbitrary disposers of the lives, liberties, or fortunes of the people'.[3] By such action legislators 'put themselves into a state of war with the people, who are thereupon absolved from any further obedience'. Similarly the 'supreme executor' breaks his trust and dissolves the government if he 'employs the force, treasure and offices of the society to corrupt the representatives . . .; or openly pre-engages the electors' to choose candidates 'whom he has by solicitations, threats, promises or otherwise won to his designs'.[4] One of the chief points reiterated by speakers in the Convention was that the throne had become vacant through the king's own action. It could thus be argued that there was no rebellion against the king, but only that the necessary steps were being taken to provide the country with a government. Locke argued in the same way, that when prince or legislature make a bid for arbitrary power they *ipso facto* dissolve the government, so that it is they and not their subjects who 'are properly and with the greatest aggravation *rebellantes*, rebels'.[5] Locke clinched this argu-

---

[1] *Second Treatise*, §§ 214–16.   [2] § 217.   [3] § 221.
[4] § 222.   [5] § 227; cf. § 226.

ment by quotations from William Barclay,[1] admitting that there might be circumstances in which a people need not necessarily submit to tyranny, since a king who endeavours to overturn the government, or subjects his kingdom to the dominion of another, '*ipso facto* becomes no king and loses all power and regal authority over his people'.[2]

Locke could thus show that even 'the great champion of absolute monarchy' admitted that rulers might forfeit their subjects' allegiance. But he was no radical, like Milton. Milton, arguing, like Locke, that 'the power of kings and magistrates is nothing else, but what is only derivative, transferred and committed to them in trust from the people to the common good of them all',[3] had concluded that the people could choose or reject a king, 'retain him or depose him, though no tyrant, merely by the liberty and right of free-born men to be governed as seems to them best'.[4] The people, according to Locke's theory, have 'the supreme power', but this is no popular sovereignty, for it is normally in abeyance, and 'can never take place till the government be dissolved'.[5] While a society lasts, he repeats in his concluding paragraph, 'the power that every individual gave the society when he entered into it, can never revert to the individuals again, . . . but will always remain in the community'; and similarly, when the society has established a permanent system of government, 'the legislative can never revert to the people whilst that government lasts, because, having provided a legislative with power to continue for ever, they have given up their political power to

[1] A Scottish writer of the sixteenth century who had upheld the divine right of kings against Buchanan and other contemporary opponents of absolute monarchy.

[2] §§ 232, 233, 235–8.

[3] J. Milton, *The Tenure of Kings and Magistrates* (1649), in *Prose Works* (Bohn's edn.), ii. 11.

[4] Ibid., p. 14.   [5] *Second Treatise*, § 149.

the legislative and cannot resume it'. It 'reverts to the society' only 'if they have set limits to the duration of their legislative, . . . or else when by the miscarriages of those in authority it is forfeited'.[1]

Locke emphasized that he did not expect this to happen frequently, and protested that he ought not to be accused of 'laying a ferment for frequent rebellion'. People are naturally too inert to be easily stirred to insurrection, so that 'revolutions happen not upon every little mismanagement in public affairs'. In reality, he urged, people are more likely to revolt if they are made miserable by exposure 'to the ill-usage of arbitrary power', and the knowledge that a government which abuses its power will forfeit it 'is the best fence against rebellion, and the probablest means to hinder it'.[2] Locke was no democrat, and it would never have occurred to him that the best method of securing a due sense of responsibility in governments is the mechanism of popular representation. In this, as in every other aspect of his political theory, he simply accepted the underlying assumptions of the English constitution of his day. In the last resort, if this broke down, the people could 'appeal to Heaven'. In 1688 this ordeal had fortunately been avoided; but they might have had to submit the justice of their cause to the God of battles, as they had done, in Locke's childhood, in the Civil War.

Locke's work was hailed, as no doubt it was intended to be, as a controversial work in justification of the Revolution. As such it was attacked by the enemies of the Revolution, and though it found some supporters at once,[3]

---

[1] *Second Treatise*, § 243.   [2] §§ 223–6.

[3] Apart from James Tyrrell, who published an abbreviation of a work by Richard Cumberland under the title *A Brief Disquisition of the Law of Nature* (1692), and a lengthy analysis of the English constitution, entitled *Bibliotheca Politica* (1694), Locke's views were upheld by William Molyneux, who applied them in a work entitled *The Case of Ireland's being Bound by Acts of*

the Whig leaders themselves seem to have hesitated at first about accepting it.¹ Tory circles not unnaturally resented such devastating criticism of the doctrines they had been brought up to regard as sacred.² Locke never regained his studentship at Christ Church, of which he had been deprived in 1684, and though it seems that he would have liked to return to Oxford,³ it may be doubted whether he would have found a friendly atmosphere there. Even after his death an Oxford letter-writer declared: 'I think that both Locke and my Lord Shaftesbury were as arrant atheists as Spinoza, and more corrupt than any sect of the heathen philosophers.'⁴ Another writer described him as Arian and Socinian, and nearly thirty years later Thomas Hearne recorded in his diary that he had never had a very good opinion of Locke, 'who, though a man of parts, was however a man of very bad principles. Mr. Lock, indeed, hath been cried up and magnified by a set of men of Republican principles, but Orthodox and truly honest men have detected his errors and fallacies and endeavoured what they could to obstruct his infection'.⁵

Parliament in England stated (Dublin, 1698), and corresponded with Locke on this subject. Another admirer of Locke was a friend of Molyneux's, Robert Molesworth, who was English ambassador at Copenhagen, and on his return in 1694 published an *Account of Denmark as it was in the Year 1692*. With its praise of liberty and denunciation of popery and divine right, and its reference to the 'fundamental constitution of the country', this work is characteristically Whiggish, if not specifically Lockian, in tone.

¹ Ch. Bastide, *John Locke, ses théories politiques et leur influence en Angleterre* (Paris, 1906), p. 262.

² Not that Filmer's influence was immediately extinguished by Locke's attack, for some of his writings were reissued in 1696.

³ According to Lord King, he petitioned the king for his studentship to be restored, but there were difficulties in the way and nothing was done (*Life of John Locke*, p. 175).

⁴ Letter from John Hutton to Dr. Charlett, President of Trinity, 4 Feb. 1706, quoted in Bastide, op. cit., p. 283.

⁵ Ibid., p. 284. On the charge of Socinianism, see p. 219, below.

Such ill odour in Tory nostrils Locke no doubt owed largely to the laxity of his churchmanship and his support of toleration, which had immediately involved him in an acrid controversy; but, even if he had been the friend of Shaftesbury, it was absurdly unjust to call him an atheist. At the same time, of course, the question of toleration was itself an issue of party politics, and the writers who attacked Locke for upholding it were attacking the man who supported the Revolution. These, perhaps, were only the extremists and irreconcilables, but even more moderate Tories, who had joined the Whigs in repudiating James II, tried to avoid having to endorse the more definitely Whiggish formulae propounded in the Convention. They resisted any phraseology which might imply that the monarchy was not hereditary, and if they accepted William III, they did so because he was king *de facto*.[1]

Except that he endeavoured to assist the passage of the Toleration Act,[2] Locke's share in the Revolution itself was not that of an active participant; but the king thought highly of him, and offered him the embassy in Brandenburg, and later that at Vienna. Locke declined these offers on grounds of health, but he finally accepted a minor government appointment at home (he became a member of the body of commissioners who heard appeals in prize cases), and in 1696 he was appointed to a seat on the Council of Trade and Plantations. For a few years after the Revolution he maintained a fairly close association with

[1] According to Burnet, some of the clergy who rejected the notion of an elective king were prepared to recognize William's title as a conqueror (*History of his Own Time*, iv. 824). See also G. M. Straka, *Anglican Reaction to the Revolution of 1688* (Madison, Wisconsin, 1962).

[2] What Locke hoped for was a 'comprehension' act as well as an act of 'indulgence' to dissenters, and he was disappointed when the former had to be dropped owing to the hostility of the Anglican clergy (cf. his letter to Limborch, quoted in Fox Bourne, *Life of John Locke*, ii. 150).

public affairs. He developed a lively interest in monetary and other economic questions, on which he wrote several pamphlets, and when the question of renewing the Licensing Act was debated in parliament in 1695, he contributed a paper which seems to have had a considerable influence on the decision to allow freedom of printing. For a time he took an active part in the proceedings of the Council of Trade, but his health was too frail for the work and visits to London which this involved, and his remaining years, until his death in 1704, he spent in the country, engaged in study and literary work. His political doctrines had been slow at first to win acceptance, but their influence gained ground in course of time, until in the eighteenth century they were almost universally acknowledged as the explanation of the Glorious Revolution, and of the constitution that rested on it.[1]

[1] Even Bolingbroke, for example, jettisoned divine right in his *Idea of a Patriot King* (1738).

VII

POLITICAL TRUSTEESHIP

In the penetrating Introduction to his translation of Otto Gierke's *Political Theories of the Middle Age*, and more fully in an article entitled 'Trust and Corporation',[1] F. W. Maitland drew attention to the importance in English political theory and practice of the idea of the trust. His main concern was to show how this concept of private law has served as a valuable and peculiarly English substitute for a regular law of corporations, but he also alluded briefly to the subject with which this study deals—the application of the trust concept to the powers and duties of government itself. 'In the course of the eighteenth century', he wrote,[2] 'it became a parliamentary commonplace that "all political power is a trust"; and this is now so common a commonplace that we seldom think over it. But it was useful. Applied to the kingly power it gently relaxed that royal chord in our polity which had been racked to the snapping point by Divine right and State religion.' It conveyed 'the suggestion of a duty, enforceable indeed, but rather as a matter of "good conscience" than as a matter of "strict law" . . .; the supposition that God was the author of the trust was not excluded, and the idea of trust was extremely elastic.'

'Open an English newspaper', he wrote further,[3] 'and

---

[1] Reprinted in *Collected Papers* (Cambridge, 1911), iii. 321–404, and again in *Selected Essays* (Cambridge, 1936), pp. 141–222.

[2] *Political Theories of the Middle Age*, p. xxxvi.

[3] *Collected Papers*, iii. 403.

you will be unlucky if you do not see the word "trustee" applied to "the Crown" or to some high and mighty body. I have just made the experiment, and my lesson for to-day is, that as the Transvaal has not yet received a representative constitution, the Imperial parliament is "a trustee for the colony". There is metaphor here. Those who speak thus would admit that the trust was not one which any court could enforce, and might say that it was only a "moral" trust.' But, he continued, legal metaphors are worth study, especially when they have become political commonplaces, and it is not always easy to say where metaphor begins. The trust concept is as common today as when Maitland wrote, if not commoner, and my object in this study is to examine the origins of this political metaphor, and its place in the history of English political thought.

It is commonly associated with Locke's *Treatise of Civil Government*, though not all commentators on Locke have fully appreciated the implications of his use of it, and some have treated it as merely a variety of the theory of contract. Maitland himself remarked that 'the introduction of talk about trusts into such works as Locke's serves to conceal some of the weak points in the contractual theory of government',[1] and Gierke appears to have regarded Locke's theory as essentially identical with that of the contract. The late Professor C. E. Vaughan pointed out the difference between the contract and the trust as it appears in Locke,[2] and this was further emphasized by Sir Ernest Barker;[3] but he left untouched the question of

[1] *Political Theories of the Middle Age*, p. xxxvi, n. 3.
[2] In *Studies in the History of Political Philosophy before and after Rousseau* (Manchester, 1925), i. 145 ff.
[3] In the notes to his translation of Gierke, *Natural Law and the Theory of Society* (Cambridge, 1934), ii. 299. See also the Introduction to his *Social Contract* (Oxford, 1947), pp. xxvi–xxx.

the origin of the trust idea, and in writing of 'Locke's theory of the political trust'[1] he appeared to attribute it mainly, if not entirely, to Locke.

Locke was so popular and widely read a writer in the eighteenth century that one is naturally inclined to ascribe the vogue of the trust concept to its being borrowed from him. But the idea of trust was also very common in the seventeenth century, and while it is possible that eighteenth-century writers took it from Locke rather than from other authors, it is clear that it was already a political commonplace before Locke's time. It may be of interest, therefore, to examine some other examples of its use, and attempt some discussion of the implications of the whole idea. My researches do not pretend to be at all exhaustive, and have indeed been largely confined to fairly obvious and easily accessible sources. I might have found some better examples, but these have yielded a varied harvest, which is amply abundant for the purpose.

According to Maitland the political trust is a metaphor from the private law of trusts. But the legal or, to be accurate, equitable trust itself is only a special and technical application of the meaning of the word 'trust' to the case of the man who is 'trusted' to apply the property vested or confided in him on behalf of the beneficiary. The development of the Court of Chancery turned what was originally an obligation on the conscience of the trustee into as legally binding an obligation as a duty imposed by common law or statute; but when trusts first came into practice no doubt they were so called because it was felt that the essence of them was the trust or confidence reposed by the trustor in the trustee. If we turn to the political trust, we shall find that many of the instances in which it occurs are so phrased as to leave no doubt that the writer clearly had

[1] Op. cit., ii. 349.

the analogy of the legal trust in mind. But there are other instances in which this is not so clear, and the question arises whether they are not to be explained as a direct application of the general meaning of the word trust, without any conscious legal metaphor from the trust in its technical sense.[1]

Let us take, to begin with, the very common phrase 'an office or place of trust'. This is applied to a great variety of positions and duties, political and otherwise, sometimes quite generally in the sense of a position the occupant of which has confidence placed in him, and is required therefore to be a person who can be trusted;[2] but it often conveys also the sense of responsibility, with emphasis on the duties to be discharged, and in this way it approaches the legal idea of the obligation to act on someone else's behalf. When we find the Attorney-General in 1629 described as 'an officer of trust and secrecy',[3] the word 'trust' is clearly equivalent to trustworthiness, and the same sense occurs again in the fifth of the Ten Propositions (1641), which demands that 'some persons of public trust, and well-affected in religion', should supervise the education of the royal family.[4]

It is only a short step from 'an *officer* of trust' to 'an *office* of trust', and though the meaning of the word is now changed, it does not necessarily become a legal metaphor. There is no specially legal reference, for example, in a number of passages in the Grand Remonstrance (1641), among them the well-known request that 'your Majesty

[1] I hoped that the *Oxford English Dictionary* might be helpful, but it throw no light on this particular question.

[2] Compare with this, too, the common address to a man appointed to some public position as 'trusty and well-beloved'.

[3] S. R. Gardiner, *Constitutional Documents of the Puritan Revolution* (3rd edn., Oxford, 1906), p. 93.

[4] Ibid., p. 165.

will vouchsafe to employ such persons in your great and public affairs, and to take such to be near you in places of trust, as your Parliament may have cause to confide in';[1] or the allusion later in the same document to those who sought to 'gain to themselves and their parties the places of greatest trust and power in the kingdom'.[2] We may compare with these some passages from Cromwell's speeches. As we shall see, Cromwell was continually using the trust concept, most frequently in a sense clearly involving the idea of obligation, and often with an evident sense of the metaphor from legal obligation, so that one cannot be certain that it was not always present in his mind. Still, when he refers to 'competition for any place of real and signal trust',[3] the meaning seems to be just a general one of responsibility. What Cromwell meant by a place of trust may be gathered from some remarks in Speech XIII on the 'qualifications that persons must be qualified with, that are put into places of Public office and Trust',[4] for he observes that 'an Office of Trust is a very large word; it goeth almost to a Constable, if not altogether;—it goeth far'. In Speech XI, also, he tells us 'I was a person that, from my first employment, was suddenly preferred and lifted up from lesser trusts to greater; from my first being a Captain of a Troop of Horse'.[5] He goes on to say, with an evident sense of obligation, 'I did labour as well as I could to discharge my trust', but this need not necessarily imply a conscious metaphor from the legal trust.

[1] Gardiner, p. 205.

[2] Ibid., p. 207; cf. also pp. 204, 224, 231, 319, 349. In another passage (p. 220), where the nobility were 'sensible of the duty and trust which belongs to them', the word seems to be equivalent to responsibility.

[3] T. Carlyle (ed. S. C. Lomas), *The Letters and Speeches of Oliver Cromwell*, ii. 282.   [4] Ibid., iii. 111.

[5] Ibid., p. 64. For further illustrations of Cromwell's idea of trust cf. ibid. ii. 299, 354; iii. 332.

The phrase 'an office or place of trust', or some closely similar expression, came into almost regular use for any kind of public employment, national or municipal. It occurs (to take a few examples) in the Corporation Act (1661), in both Test Acts (1673 and 1678), and in the Act of Settlement (1701), and duly reappears in the nineteenth century in the Act repealing the Test and Corporation Acts, and in the Roman Catholic Emancipation Act. In all these acts the meaning seems to be the same as in the passages from the Grand Remonstrance quoted above, that of an office of responsibility, calling for a trustworthy holder, but with no conscious or special reference to the obligation of legal trusteeship.

Closely parallel with this usage is that found in the king's complaint in 1642 that parliament was attempting 'to dispossess many of our ancient nobility of the command and trust reposed in them by us', and to appoint others 'who cannot be properly serviceable to the counties wherewith they are entrusted'; the sheriff therefore was to issue warrants 'according to the trust reposed in him by our said Commission'.[1] The meaning here is clearly the straightforward one of confidence or reliance, and may be paralleled, for example, by a much earlier commission of lieutenancy (1585), which refers to 'this our service in our said counties . . . committed to your fidelity', or the phraseology used in 1599 in appointing an admiral, who is said to be chosen 'to commit so great a trust and charge unto'.[2]

[1] Gardiner, pp. 259, 260.

[2] Prothero, *Select Statutes and Constitutional Documents* (4th edn., Oxford, 1913), pp. 155, 164. A similar use of the word occurs in Spenser's *Faerie Queene* (1596), v. iv. 2:

> Therefore whylome to knights of great emprise
> The charge of Justice given was in trust
> That they might execute her judgments wise.

We may turn next to an interesting group of passages connected with the impeachment of Buckingham in 1626, where, besides such phrases as 'persons eminent in wisdom and trust', or 'offices . . . both carefully and sufficiently executed by several persons of such wisdom, trust and ability',[1] we find a statement that it was an undoubted right of parliament 'to question and complain of all persons . . . found grievous to the commonwealth, in abusing the power and trust committed to them by their sovereign'.[2] Here the meaning is still one of confidence, but the added suggestion of its breach or abuse begins to point in the direction of the political trust as found in Locke. The same suggestion occurs farther on in the course of the impeachment, where the duke, who 'by reason of his said offices of Great Admiral . . . and by reason of the trust thereunto belonging, ought at all times . . . to have safely guarded . . . the said seas', is accused of having 'neglected the just performance of his said office and duty, and broken the said trust therewith committed unto him', and of acting contrary 'to the faith and trust in that behalf reposed'.[3] Now this was the charge in actual legal proceedings against Buckingham. But he clearly was not being accused of a breach of a legal trust proper, nor is there any reason to suppose that his accusers were charging him with this even metaphorically: the charge was simply one of breach of faith, or neglect of duty. Cromwell, I think, had the same idea in mind when he declared that he would be 'false to the trust that God hath placed in me, and to the interest of the people of these nations', if he parted with his position as Protector,[4] or that he knew by experience

[1] Gardiner, p. 8.
[2] Ibid., p. 6.
[3] Ibid., pp. 10, 15.
[4] Carlyle, ii. 354.

'what troubles and difficulties do befall men under such trusts and in such undertakings'.[1]

Unmistakable examples of the political trust are common in Cromwell, as we shall see later, but the passages just cited are most instructive as to the process of thought by which the political trust came to acquire its vogue. They do not exclude the possibility that it was a conscious legal metaphor, and indeed it did come to be that. But it seems at least equally possible that the idea arose, independently at first of the legal trust, as an extension of the general meaning of trust or confidence, with the cognate idea of duty and responsibility.

After these preliminaries let us examine a selection of instances of the more fully developed political trust itself. We shall find two main forms, with some minor varieties: first, the idea that the king, or the executive, is a trustee for the people governed, and second, that members of parliament are trustees for the electorate. Sir Ernest Barker pointed out that whereas the legal trust proper involves three parties—trustor, trustee, and beneficiary (or *cestui que trust*)—in the political trust there are only two, the people being both trustor and beneficiary.[2] This was apropos of the trust-relationship between people and legislature in Locke, but the same is true of the other form of the political trust, between people and king or executive, which is also prominent in Locke. Locke's theory, in fact, contains such good examples of both forms of the political trust that, even if he is not the source of it, we may well take his statement of it as our central point, and work up to and forward from him.[3]

[1] Ibid., iii. 128, referring to the title of king offered him in the Humble Petition and Advice. Cf. also ibid. 32, 37, 162.

[2] Notes to Gierke, *Natural Law and the Theory of Society*, ii. 299; *Social Contract*, p. xxix.

[3] An interesting anticipation of the principle of trusteeship that was to be

Locke's theory of the state, it will be remembered, involves first of all a social contract or compact by which the free individuals of the state of nature consent and agree to form a political society. Subsequently to this first agreement, the people erect a legislature to have the supreme power over them, while the executive (unless it is placed in the hands of a person who, like the king of England, also has a share in the legislative power) is 'visibly subordinate and accountable to the legislature'.[1] While the legislature, or legislative, as Locke calls it, is said to be supreme, yet its power 'in the utmost bounds of it is limited to the public good of the society',[2] for 'the community put the legislative power into such hands as they think fit, with this trust, that they shall be governed by declared laws',[3] and government is 'entrusted with this condition and for this end, that men might have and secure their properties'.[4] The whole implications of Locke's theory are brought out in a later passage, where the legislative power is described as 'only a fiduciary power to act for certain ends', so that 'there remains still in the people a supreme power to remove or alter the legislative, when they find the legislative act contrary to the trust reposed in them. For all power given with trust for the attaining an end being limited by that end, whenever that end is manifestly neglected or opposed, the trust must necessarily be forfeited, and the power devolve into the hands of those that

worked out in more detail in the *Second Treatise* is to be found in Locke's early *Essay concerning Toleration* (1667), printed in Fox Bourne's *Life of John Locke* (1876), i. 174. Here 'the whole trust, power and authority of the magistrate' is said to be 'vested in him for no other purpose but to be made use of for the good, preservation, and peace of men in that society over which he is set'.

[1] *Second Treatise*, § 152.
[2] § 135.   [3] § 136.
[4] § 139. Cf. also § 142, where he writes of the bounds 'which the trust that is put in them by the society and the law of God and of Nature have set to the legislative power of every commonwealth'.

gave it, who may place it anew where they shall think best for their safety and security.'[1]

Passing to the powers and duties of the executive, Locke first discusses his function of summoning and dismissing the legislature, and this, he declares, 'gives not the executive a superiority over it, but is a fiduciary trust placed in him for the safety of the people'. The disadvantages of 'constant, frequent meetings of the legislative' led the people 'to entrust' this function to the executive, but, like the legislative power itself, it was not to be 'an arbitrary power depending on his good pleasure, but with this trust always to have it exercised only for the public weal'.[2] Should the executive use the force at his disposal 'to hinder the meeting and acting of the legislative, . . . without authority, and contrary to the trust put in him', he would be in 'a state of war with the people, who have a right to reinstate their legislative in the exercise of their power'.[3]

An executive not separate from the legislature, but sharing in it as the king of England does, has 'a double trust put in him, both to have a part in the legislative and the supreme execution of the laws', and he 'acts against both when he goes about to set up his own arbitrary will as the law of the society'.[4] The legislature also acts contrary to its trust if it endeavours to seize arbitrary power for itself,[5] and such breach of trust, on the part of the executive or of the legislature, involves the dissolution of the government. It is for the people to decide whether either the prince or legislature act contrary to their trust; 'for who shall be judge whether his trustee or deputy acts well

[1] § 149.   [2] § 156.
[3] § 153. Cf. his application of the trust concept to the prerogative, §§ 160, 161, 164, 167.
[4] § 222.   [5] § 221.

and according to the trust reposed in him, but he who deputes him, and must, by having deputed him, have still a power to discard him when he fails in his trust?'[1]

Here, and in a number of similar passages scattered through the *Second Treatise of Government*, we have the whole doctrine of the political trust in its two main branches; and whether Locke was aware of it or not, it is interesting to observe how his language betrays the fact that the political trust is not on all fours with the legal trust proper. First, it will be noticed how, in the passage just quoted, he introduces, almost casually, the word 'deputy' as an alternative to 'trustee'; yet thereby he is really importing a quite different notion from that of trusteeship.[2] Another significant phrase, though again it is introduced almost incidentally, occurs in a passage where Locke remarks that political power is given 'to the governors whom the society hath set over itself, with this *express or tacit* trust [my italics], that it shall be employed for their good and the preservation of their property'.[3] This at once suggests a doubt in Locke's mind whether the political trust had ever been expressly established at any time in the history of a state; and one wonders whether he would not have admitted that the political trust was only a metaphor. One is reminded of his argument that though individuals could only become members of a state and be subject to its government by their own consent, yet that consent might be a tacit consent, implied by their continued residence within its territories.[4]

---

[1] *Second Treatise*, § 240; cf. § 242.

[2] Why he does so is fairly obvious; it is in order to argue more plausibly that a defaulting government may be removed. This passage is also of interest in that it almost exactly echoes the thought of Bishop Ponet (cf. below, p. 166).

[3] § 171.

[4] § 119. On the relation between trust and contract see below, p. 166.

The discussion of the origins and development of the metaphor of the trust will be clearer if we take the trusteeship of the legislature separately from that of the executive or king, and it will be convenient to take the latter first. The idea that the possession of power involved a responsibility for its proper use was a commonplace of medieval political thought, which was often expressed in terms of the necessity for a king's actions to be ruled by respect for law, or again of the subordination of positive law to the law of nature or the law of God. On occasions, as in the baronial movements of the thirteenth century, or in the deposition of Richard II, the feeling that a king was neglecting his duty or abusing his power would lead his subjects to claim a right to put pressure on him. Seventeenth-century politicians looked back to these episodes as precedents for their own action, and the persistence of this medieval tradition, which was a marked feature of seventeenth-century political thought in England, may well have contributed to the development of the idea of political trusteeship.[1]

It was with the rise of the notion of popular sovereignty, however, that the phraseology of trust began to appear as

[1] This, I think, is as far as one can safely go. In his *Constitutional History of Medieval England* J. E. A. Jolliffe wrote of 'the belief that almost all men of learning held—that the king was trustee for the law which must itself determine his actions' (p. 260; cf. pp. 287, 486). Now John of Salisbury, whom Jolliffe quoted (p. 205) as holding that the power of kings is 'a trust for the execution of justice', writes of the *princeps* as *legis nexibus absolutus* yet as *publicae . . . utilitatis minister et aequitatis servus* (*Policraticus*, iv. 2; cf. Carlyle, *Med. Pol. Thought in the West*, ii. 15–18, for references to other medieval authorities who held that law must be tested by *aequitas*). The word *aequitas* here may suggest a connection with the chancellor's jurisdiction in whose hands English equity and trusteeship developed, and in principle its function as a corrective of the common law was indeed similar to that here ascribed to *aequitas*. But *aequitas*, which is probably best translated by some general word such as 'justice', was much older than the English trust, which had not yet developed in private law. The Middle Ages certainly had a firm belief in the responsibility of monarchy, but I feel doubtful of the propriety of interpreting this in terms of trusteeship.

a mode of expressing a responsibility of rulers not so much to God or to law as to their subjects themselves. The earliest example I have discovered of this is in Bishop Ponet's *Short Treatise of Politike Power* (1556), where after declaring that 'kings, princes and governors have their authority of the people', he asks whether any man is 'so unreasonable to deny that the whole may do as much as they have permitted one member to do, or those that have appointed an office upon trust have not authority upon just occasion (as the abuse of it) to take away that they gave? All laws do agree,' he continues, 'that men may revoke their proxies and letters of attorney when it pleaseth them, much more when they see their proctors and attorneys abuse it.'[1] Ponet was guilty of some confusion here, as is evident from the reasons he gives for this trust being revocable by the people, for he equates the trust with two other legal concepts, the proxy and the power of attorney, which are really distinct both from it and from each other.

When the development of political discontent under the Stuarts led from the assertion of parliamentary privilege to attacks on royal policy itself, the trust concept began to be freely applied to the king's position. In the Grand Remonstrance the Commons declared that their intention was not 'to lay any blemish upon your royal person, but only to represent how your royal authority and trust have been abused';[2] six months later they no longer merely blamed the king's ministers for misusing the powers entrusted to them by the king, but were prepared to regard the king himself as a defaulting trustee. In their Declaration in defence of the Militia Ordinance, asking 'if the king shall refuse to discharge that duty and trust, whether there is

---

[1] W. S. Hudson, *John Ponet* (Chicago, 1942), p. 107.
[2] Gardiner, p. 303.

not a power in the two Houses to provide for the safety of
the Parliament and peace of the kingdom', they proceeded
to require all the king's subjects to obey the orders of
parliament, 'and what they do therein is . . . to be interpreted to be done in aid of the king, in discharge of that
trust which he is tied to perform'.[1] A few days before this,
parliament had declared that kings were bound to give
their assent to bills sent up to them from both houses,
because of their coronation oath, and 'in justice they are
obliged thereunto in respect of the trust reposed in them,
which is as well to preserve the kingdom by the making
of new laws, where there shall be need, as by observing
of laws already made'.[2] Perhaps the most remarkable instance of parliament's use of this kind of terminology is in
one of three resolutions passed by both houses on 20 May
1642, in that it exactly anticipates the arguments of the
Whigs in 1689: 'That whensoever the king maketh war
upon the parliament, it is a breach of the trust reposed in
him by his people, contrary to his oath, and tending to the
dissolution of this government.'[3]

The king's reply to these contentions took the form
which he was to maintain steadily right up to the scaffold.
He did not repudiate the idea of his trusteeship, but only the
argument that it meant responsibility to parliament. Did
not the people who elected the Commons, he asked, 'look
upon them as a body but temporary and dissoluble at our
pleasure? And can it be believed that they intended them
for our guardians and controllers in the managing of that
trust which God and the law hath granted to us?'[4] After

[1] Gardiner, pp. 256, 257.
[2] Quoted in J. W. Allen, *English Political Thought, 1603–1660*, i. (1603–44),
p. 394.   [3] *Parly. Hist.*, ii. 1241.
[4] Allen, p. 409. In the Ship-money case in 1638 Sir Robert Berkeley had
argued that it was a 'maxim of the law of England' that 'the King is a person
trusted with the state of the commonwealth' (Gardiner, p. 122).

the civil war these continued to be the positions taken up by both sides. Parliament declared that the king had broken his trust to parliament and the kingdom, and was in fact a traitor; the king replied that in all he had done he had endeavoured to fulfil the trust given him by God.[1] At the king's trial itself the idea of his trusteeship played a leading part in the proceedings. The charge against the king asserted that he was 'trusted with a limited power to govern by and according to the laws of the land and not otherwise', and that 'by his trust, oath and office' he was 'obliged to use the power committed to him for the good and benefit of the people and for the preservation of their rights', but that he had had 'a wicked design to erect and uphold in himself an unlimited and tyrannical power . . . against the public interest, common right, liberty, justice and peace of the people of this nation, by and from whom he was entrusted as aforesaid'.[2]

The king denied the authority of the court to try him, and, as before, declared that his responsibility was not to parliament or the people, but to God. 'I have a trust committed to me by God,' he declared, 'by old and lawful descent. I will not betray that trust to answer to a new unlawful authority, for all the world. . . . I am entrusted with the liberty of my people, I do stand more for the liberties of my people than any one that is seated here as a judge. . . . I will never betray my trust.'[3] The king, therefore, refused to plead, and Bradshaw's long series of speeches never persuaded him to recognize the court's jurisdiction. To the end the king maintained that he could

[1] The king's contention appears, for instance, in his third answer to the Propositions of Newcastle (Gardiner, p. 314). Cf. also his letter to the Speaker of the House of Lords, ibid., p. 330.

[2] Ibid., pp. 371, 373. Similar language appears in the sentence on the king, ibid., p. 377.

[3] Quoted in J. G. Muddiman, *The Trial of Charles I*, p. 82.

not 'submit to your pretended authority without violating the trust I have from God for the welfare and liberty of my people'.[1] This being so, it was ineffective for Bradshaw merely to ring the changes, as he did over and over again, on the parliamentary contention that the king was 'but an officer in trust, and he ought to discharge that trust for the people, and if he do not they are to take order' for his 'animadversion and punishment'.[2]

This was no answer to the king's claim that he had indeed a trust, but a trust from God. Bradshaw argued, accordingly, that hereditary descent was not the only factor that determined the succession to the throne, but that 'the kings of England ever held the greatest assurance of their titles when they were declared and approved by Parliament'. The coronation oath, he urged, showed that there was 'a contract and bargain made between the king and his people, and the oath is taken for the performance, and certainly, Sir, the bond is reciprocal. . . .'[3] This talk of a contract, however, was, strictly speaking, inconsistent with the theory that the king was a trustee, and Bradshaw subsequently dropped it, to reiterate the contention that kingship was 'an office of trust'. 'Sir,' he urged finally, 'the term traitor cannot be spared, we shall easily agree it must denote and suppose a breach of trust. . . . When you did break your trust to the kingdom, you did break your trust to your superior. For the kingdom is that for which you were trusted. And therefore, Sir, for this breach of trust when you are called to account, you are called to account by your superiors.'[4]

[1] Gardiner, p. 376.
[2] Muddiman, p. 116.
[3] Ibid., p. 121.

[4] Ibid., pp. 121, 122. Bradshaw's reference to the contract theory alongside the principle of trusteeship may possibly be explained by the trust concept being associated in his mind more with what I have called the general than with the strictly legal meaning of trust, so that the inconsistency

Bradshaw's argument, that the king was an officer appointed on trust by his superiors, the people, and could be brought to account by them, which is essentially identical with the view expressed by Locke, had been led up to by a number of writers and pamphleteers on the parliamentary side. Prynne, for example, had maintained that all high officers of state were 'more the kingdom's than the king's', and that though the king normally appoints them, if he uses his powers improperly 'no doubt the Parliament may justly regulate or resume that trust so far into their own hands as to recommend faithful persons' whom the king must accept.[1] This would have supported the claim of parliament in the Grand Remonstrance to control royal appointments rather than their later claim to bring the king himself to trial; but Prynne proceeded to argue that hereditary kingdoms were 'but offices of public trust for the people's good and safety', and as 'inferior magistrates or bishops by divine institution may, on occasion, be deprived, condemned, and executed, "why not kings as well as they?"'[2] Allen did not think that Prynne meant to assert that anybody really had a right to condemn and execute

may not have struck him. This is confirmed by the address which the solicitor-general, Cook, would have delivered had the king pleaded to the charge (Muddiman, pp. 233 ff.). He asserted that 'when many families agree, for the preservation of humane society, to invest any king or governor with power and authority, there is a *mutual trust and confidence between them* [my italics] that the king shall improve his power for their good' (p. 246). Here again we seem to have the contract theory combined with a general rather than a strictly legal use of the trust idea, so that the trust is practically equated with the obligation to keep the contract. Incidentally we may notice the weakness of the argument by which Cook tried to overcome the legal difficulty of convicting the king himself of treason. 'Though there was no positive law for it to make it treason, yet it was *resolved by the best politicians* [my italics] that it was treason to break so great a trust by the fundamental constitution of the kingdom' (ibid., p. 249).

[1] W. Prynne, *The Soveraigne Power of Parliaments and Kingdoms*, quoted in Allen, op. cit., p. 442.   [2] Ibid., pp. 445, 446.

the king, and suggested that he was 'merely offering a conundrum to the believers in divine commission'; but within a few years men did not hesitate to act on the obvious conclusion from such an argument.

These views of Prynne's appeared in 1643, and the same year saw the publication of another work, Philip Hunton's *A Treatise of Monarchy*, which is of interest because, as Professor McIlwain has pointed out, it closely anticipates several features of Locke's theory.[1] The trust concept is as fundamental in Hunton's political thought as it is in Locke's.

In every state [he writes], some must be trusted, and the highest trust is in him who hath the supreme power. These two, the supreme trust, and the supreme power, are inseparable: and such as the power is, such is the trust: an absolute power supposes an absolute trust! A power allayed with the annexion of another power, as here it is, supposeth a trust of the same nature, a joint trust, yet saving the supremacy of the monarch, so far forth as it may be saved, and not be absolute, and the others' authority nullified.[2]

Thus given currency by political writers, the trust concept frequently recurred in the Putney debates in 1647, and it not only played an important part in the trial of the king, but became as it were an official theory of the commonwealth. Cromwell told the commissioners sent from Scotland to protest against the execution of the king that 'he thought a breach of trust in a king ought to be punished more than any other crime whatsoever'[3] and

---

[1] *Politica*, i (1934–5), pp. 243–73.

[2] P. Hunton, *A Treatise of Monarchy*, ii, c. 5, § 4. Cf. also such phrases (ibid.) as 'the laws of the kingdom putting all power of force and arms into his trust', or 'the power of the sword . . . must needs belong to him who is entrusted with the government, as a necessary requisite, without which he cannot perform his trust'.

[3] Burnet, *Own Time* (ed. Airy, Oxford, 1897), i. 71.

when the Rump issued a declaration of their reasons for abolishing monarchy and establishing the commonwealth they remarked that very few kings had 'performed the trust of that office with righteousness, and due care of their subjects' good'.[1] Another writer who used it, and very closely anticipated the theory of Locke, was John Milton. Like Locke, Milton attributed the foundation of society to agreement or compact between individuals, and then declared that 'the power of kings and magistrates is nothing else, but what only is derivative, transferred and committed to them in trust from the people to the common good of them all, in whom the power yet remains fundamentally, and cannot be taken from them, without a violation of their natural birthright'.[2]

The idea of royal trusteeship constantly reappears in the political disputes of the later Stuart reigns, generally in the Whiggish sense seen in Dryden's reference to the idea that 'kings are only officers in trust'.[3] It was also used, however, from time to time, in the form used by Charles I himself to justify royal power. Clarendon, for example, while denying the derivation of sovereignty from popular grant, 'whereas in truth all power was by God and Nature invested into one Man, where still as much of it remains as he hath not parted with and shared with others', went on to speak of those 'for whose benefit it was first intrusted to him'.[4] Charles II, too, when the House of Commons protested against his declaration of indulgence in 1672, told

[1] *Parly. Hist.*, iii. 1293.

[2] J. Milton, *Tenure of Kings and Magistrates* (1649), in *Prose Works*, ed. Bohn, ii. 11. The trust concept was also used by the Rev. George Lawson, who, as Mr. A. H. Maclean has pointed out (*Camb. Hist. Journal*, ix. no. 1 (1947), pp. 69–77), anticipated many of Locke's characteristic theories. Later, it occurs in James Tyrrell's *Patriarcha non Monarcha* (1681), and in many other political writings of this period.

[3] *Absalom and Achitophel*, l. 766.

[4] Clarendon, *A Brief View and Survey of . . . Leviathan* (1670), p. 72.

them that he had never thought of using 'his power in ecclesiasticks' 'otherwise than as it hath been entrusted in him, to the peace and establishment of the Church of England, and the ease of all his subjects in general'.[1]

Political pamphlets published during the crises of the Exclusion Bill and the Revolution show that these different aspects of the trust concept were being kept constantly in play. Thus, when a Tory declared that 'it is not to be denied but that our kings have in a great measure been intrusted with the power of calling and declaring the dissolutions of parliaments', he was answered by a Whig with the question, 'Have they so? Whose trustees are they? When did they first obtain this favour?' to which the Tory rejoinder was that this was a natural right inherent in the Crown.[2] The issue between the two sides is very clearly put in a pamphlet by William Assheton, *The Royal Apology, or an Answer to the Rebel's Plea* (1684).[3] It opens by citing the common Whig belief that 'the power which kings and princes have was derived unto them from the people by way of pact or contract', and that by his coronation oath the king was 'obliged to use the power, trust and office then committed to him for the good and benefit of the people'. On the contrary, the writer argues, the king is king before his coronation, from the moment of his accession, and it is God who gave him his trust, and to whom alone he must render an account for the management of it.

[1] Grant Robertson, *Select Statutes, Cases and Documents*, p. 78.

[2] *Reflections on a pamphlet stiled 'A just and modest vindication of the proceedings of the two last Parliaments'*, by the Author of the Address to the Freemen and Freeholders of the Nation (1683). The author of this was Edmund Bohun. Cf. the Lord Chief Justice's declaration in the case of *Godden* v. *Hales* (1686) that the dispensing power was 'not a trust invested in, or granted to the king by the people, but the ancient remains of the sovereign power and prerogative of the kings of England' (Grant Robertson, p. 387).

[3] *The Rebel's Plea*, by Thomas Tomkins, was itself an answer to Baxter's *Holy Commonwealth*.

The king may indeed be described as 'an officer of trust', provided it is understood 'that the word *trust* do only refer to Almighty God, but not to the people', and provided it is not interpreted as implying a derivation of the king's authority from the people by any pact or contract.[1]

Tory writers entirely repudiated the original contract, but it is evident that they hesitated to reject the trust concept also, for had they done so they might have been accused of holding that the king had no responsibility whatever. It was a neat escape to follow Charles I in accepting the principle of trusteeship, but making God the trustor instead of the people. Another line of defence had been taken up in Cleveland's pamphlet, *Majestas Intemerata, or the Immortality of the King* (1649, reprinted in 1689), arguing that 'could it appear, the king were originally but a grand Trustee, he could not be commanded to resign that Trust; it is so a Power given away, which no reservation for its time can fetch back, nor no condition not created with it can defeat'.[2] But this, which was hardly consistent with trusteeship at all, must have been a much weaker and less effective position than that of turning trusteeship into a form of divine right itself. It did not suffice, at any rate, to avert the Revolution, which was justified on the basis of trusteeship, although the 'original contract' played a more prominent part. In this connexion, one of the most interesting contributions to the debates in the Convention was made by Serjeant (later Chief Justice) Holt, at the free conference between the Commons and the Lords on the word 'abdicated'. He knew that the political trust was not strictly a legal trust,

[1] *The Royal Apology*, pp. 2–4, 42, 53. The pamphlet is interesting also as further evidence of the loose combination of the trust concept with the contract.

[2] *Majestas Intemerata*, p. 38. A similar idea of irrevocability appears on p. 12.

but, as a lawyer, he evidently had the legal trust in mind, and made a deliberate extension of it. The Lords wanted to substitute 'deserted' for 'abdicated', because they thought abdication implied a formal deed of renunciation, such as James II had never executed. Holt argued that

both in the common law of England, and the civil law, and in common understanding, there are express acts of renunciation that are not by deed; for . . . the government and magistracy is under a trust, and any acting contrary to that trust is a renouncing of the trust, though it be not a renouncing by formal deed: for it is a plain declaration, by act and deed, though not in writing, that he who hath the trust, acting contrary, is a disclaimer of the trust; especially . . . if the actings be such as are inconsistent with, and subversive of this trust: for how can a man, in reason or sense, express a greater renunciation of a trust, than by the constant declarations of his actions to be quite contrary to that trust?[1]

Another typical example of the use to which the trust concept was put at the time of the Revolution may be seen in Robert Ferguson's pamphlet, *A Brief Justification of the Prince of Orange's Descent into England* (1689). Our ancestors, he argued, 'delegated' the executive functions of government to the king 'as a Trust, which he is to swear faithfully to perform', and reserved to themselves the power 'of inspecting his administration, making him responsible for it, and of abdicating him from the sovereignty upon universal and egregious failures in the Trust that had been credited and consigned to him'.[2]

Turning now to the idea of the trusteeship of the legislature, we shall be struck by the fact that though Elizabeth's parliaments sometimes chafed under the restrictions

[1] *Parly. Hist.*, v. 71.
[2] *A Brief Justification*, p. 15. Further references to the principle of royal trusteeship occur on pp. 17, 18, and 19.

imposed on them by her government, it did not (so far as I have discovered) occur to them to describe themselves as trustees for the people. But the accession of James I was soon followed by far-reaching constitutional disputes between king and parliament, in which the trust concept came to be freely used. As early as 1604 the king's proclamation that election writs should be returned to Chancery and disputed elections decided there led to a determined stand by the Commons on behalf of their privileges, and in the course of their Apology (June 20) they put first among the three things in which, they declared, 'the rights and liberties of the Commons of England' chiefly consisted, 'that the shires, cities and boroughs of England, by representation to be present, have free choice of such persons as they shall put in trust to represent them'.[1] Six years later, when various grievances were being ventilated, the Commons declared in their petition to the king: 'We . . . have thought it to appertain to our duties, as well toward your Majesty as to those that have trusted us and sent us to their service, to present unto your Majesty's view these fears and griefs of your people.'[2]

Now the expression 'put in trust', used in 1604, seems like a legal metaphor, but the 'trusted' of 1610 is more like an instance of what I have called the general than of the special legal sense of trust. This is confirmed by the fact that in a speech to parliament in 1610 the king himself had used the word in the same connexion, when he warned the members that they must be faithful to himself and 'to your countries that trust and employ you'.[3] A comparison of these passages confirms the view already suggested, that while the political trust came to be a legal metaphor, its development owed something to the currency of the word 'trust', whether verb or noun, in its general sense of having

[1] Prothero, p. 289.   [2] Ibid., p. 306.   [3] Ibid., p. 294.

confidence in someone. It is also significant that it was during the sixteenth and seventeenth centuries that the equitable trust came to be a common institution in England,[1] and greater public familiarity with the idea and practice of trusteeship in private affairs may well explain the giving of a definitely legal complexion to the general idea of trust or confidence in politics.[2] The legal aspect of the political trust probably also derived confirmation from Coke, who described parliament as being 'trusted for the commonwealth', so that they must 'perform the trust reposed in them'.[3]

It was with the meeting of the Long Parliament, as we have seen, that the trust concept was first freely applied to the position of the king, and the Commons continued to make frequent use of the idea of their own trusteeship as the basis for their policy. Thus, in the instructions proposed by the House of Commons for the committee in Scotland (1641), they declared that if the king would not accept their demands 'we shall be forced, in discharge of the trust which we owe to the State, and to those whom we represent, to resolve upon' suitable methods for the defence of Ireland.[4] Here it will be observed that parliament, consonantly with its increasing encroachment on the sovereignty of the king, claimed a wider responsibility than that merely to their constituents; and in the propositions presented to the king in the negotiations for the Treaty of Oxford (1643) they spoke of 'the duty which

[1] Cf. Holdsworth, *History of English Law*, v. 304 ff.

[2] Another instance of what I may call a transitional use of the word trust about this time occurs in Whitelock's speech in parliament on the subject of impositions (2 July 1610), when he argued that 'the power of imposing hath so great a trust in it . . . that it hath ever been ranked among those rights of sovereign power' (Prothero, p. 351).

[3] Coke, *Institutes*, iv (published in 1641), c. i, p. 44.

[4] Gardiner, p. 201.

we owe to God, your Majesty, and the kingdom, for which we are entrusted'.[1] These ideas are seen again in the proceedings at the trial of Charles I, when Bradshaw, addressing the king, remarked that 'the Commons of England assembled in Parliament' had resolved to bring him to judgement, 'according to the debt they owe to God, to Justice, the kingdom and themselves, and according to that fundamental power that is vested, and trust reposed in them by the People'.[2] Trust here could be construed in a general sense as meaning confidence, and the same is true of the idea as it appears in various pamphlets written on the parliamentary side about this time, but the more definitely legal usage was also current. An example worth quoting is in a pamphlet entitled *A Disclaimer and Answer*, dated May 1643,[3] in which the idea is made the basis for a claim to full sovereignty, not (as Allen remarks) for parliament but for the Commons alone. 'He knows nothing of the nature of Parliaments,' we read, 'that knows not that the House of Commons is absolutely entrusted with our persons and estates, and by our laws invested with a power to dispose of them as they shall think meet. . . . When we chose our knights and burgesses for the Parliament we entrusted them with all the power we could invest them withal to do whatsoever in their wisdom they should think meet.' A pamphlet called *The Contra-Replicant* (January 1643) argued that 'in all forms of government the people passes, by way of trust, all that power which it retains not',[4] thus applying the trust concept alike to a monarchy or a representative assembly. Sometimes the parliamentary

[1] Gardiner, p. 263.

[2] Quoted in Muddiman, p. 77. The trust concept was also applied to the court itself (Gardiner, p. 358).

[3] Quoted in Allen, pp. 472, 473.

[4] Quoted ibid., p. 459. Other examples of the trust concept will be found in pamphlets quoted by Allen on pp. 460, 464.

trust concept was applied to the Lords,[1] but normally it
was the representative house that was referred to in this
way, and in the Agreement of the People, as presented to
parliament on 15 January 1649, the steps that were proposed, as it were to actualize the trust, are of interest as
showing that the legal aspects of the trust concept were
clearly perceived by this time. Indentures were to be
drawn up between each representative and six or more
electors, 'expressing their election of him as a representer
of them . . . and his acceptance of that trust, and his
promise accordingly to perform the same with faithful-
ness'.[2]

When the Rump abolished monarchy and proclaimed
that England was a commonwealth, they declared that the
nation was 'to return to its just and ancient right of being
governed by its own representatives . . . from time to time
chosen and entrusted for that purpose by the people'.[3]
Cromwell, therefore, was able to convict them out of their
own mouths; the Long Parliament had been turned out,
he told the city aldermen, not 'because they were a parliament, but because they did not perform their trust'.[4] The
summons to the Barebones Parliament (June 1653) mentioned that certain persons were to be nominated 'to whom
the great charge and trust of so weighty affairs is to be
committed', and members therefore were 'to take upon
you the said trust unto which you are hereby called and
appointed'.[5] When Cromwell addressed the assembled
parliament in his first speech he emphasized the idea of
trusteeship again and again. He had besought the Rump,
he said, 'that they would be mindful of their duty to God

[1] An example of the idea applied to Lords as well as Commons is in the
Engagement between the king and the Scots of December 1647, in Gardiner,
p. 349.   [2] Ibid., pp. 364 ff.   [3] Ibid., p. 386.
[4] Carlyle, iii. 441.   [5] Gardiner, p. 405.

and men, in the discharge of the trust reposed in them',
but when they declined to 'devolve the power and trust to
some well-affected men', he considered their determination to perpetuate themselves 'an high breach of trust . . .
a breach of trust such as a greater could not be'. 'But you',
he continued, 'are men who know the Lord . . . and may
be trusted with this cause', and so he thought it advisable
to 'offer somewhat . . . as to the discharge of the trust that
is now incumbent upon you'.[1]

Cromwell recurred to the same idea when he had difficulties with the first parliament of the Protectorate, and
expressed it this time in unmistakably legal phraseology.
If 'trustees in Parliament,' he told them, should by experience find elements in the constitution that needed
alteration, he would not refuse to agree, but their duty
now was to accept the Instrument of Government and not
to criticize its fundamentals. It had been 'already submitted to the judicious, honest people of this nation. . . . And
what their judgement is, is visible by submission to it; by
acting upon it; by restraining their trustees from meddling
with it.'[2] We have seen already that Cromwell habitually
thought of any public office or responsibility in terms of
trusteeship; he applied the idea accordingly to the council
of state,[3] and constantly referred to his own position as
Protector in the same terms.[4]

By the middle of the seventeenth century, clearly, the
trust concept had become an established mode of thought.
But while always involving the idea of responsibility, it did
not necessarily connote, as in Locke, even a conditional

[1] Carlyle, ii. 279, 284, 287, 289, 290.

[2] Ibid., ii. 420. Ludlow also referred to the republican members whom
Cromwell refused to admit to parliament as being 'excluded from the discharge of their trust' (*Memoirs*, ed. Firth, ii. 18).

[3] Cf. Carlyle, ii. 374, 384; also Gardiner, pp. 384, 386, 417, 442, 462.

[4] Typical instances are Carlyle, ii. 382; iii. 20, 162, 304.

right of revolution. Even Hobbes made use of it, applying it to the possession of supreme power by the sovereign monarch or assembly.[1] Clarendon rejected Hobbes's doctrines, but though himself no friend of the parliamentary claims for which the trust concept had been a support, he found it useful as an argument against the idea of unlimited sovereignty. A ruler, he urged, must be held bound to observe 'certain rules . . . (I do not say conditions) for the better exercise of that sovereign power', even 'though there should be no oath administered for the observation thereof. . . . And if he do wilfully decline those rules, doth he not break the trust reposed in him? I do not say forfeit the trust, as if the sovereignty were at an end, but break that trust, violate that justice he should observe?'[2]

Clarendon is here protesting against the idea of irresponsible or arbitrary power, and is urging in effect that all power involves a responsibility to use it justly and rightly. That he expressed this in terms of trusteeship goes to show how common and well established the trust concept had become. It was as natural a mode of expression for Clarendon as it was in our own day for Professor Pollard, for instance, when he wrote: 'Power must always be a matter of responsibility, whether it is exercised by an individual, a parliament, or a trades-union. It is a trust, and the idea that its possessor is responsible to and for no one but himself is as pernicious for the voter as for the monarch.'[3]

One could quote numerous examples from the Restoration period of the continued vogue of the parliamentary

[1] *Leviathan*, cc. 19, 20. Filmer, too, declared that every freeholder with a vote 'ought to know with what power he trusts those whom he chooseth, because such trust is the foundation of the power of the House of Commons' (*Works*, ed. Laslett, p. 133).

[2] Clarendon, *Brief View and Survey of . . . Leviathan*, pp. 122, 123.

[3] A. F. Pollard, *The Evolution of Parliament* (1920), p. 357.

trust concept. A particularly interesting one is provided by a broadsheet of March 1660, containing draft instructions from a constituency to its members, published in the hope that many constituencies would adopt them and confront their candidates with them. The substance of it is a request to the persons 'to be elected and returned by us for our Representatives and Trustees in this approaching Parliament' to effect various specified measures 'in pursuance of the Trust reposed by us in them'.[1] Hitherto the trust concept had generally been used by parliament as an argument to justify its stand against the royal prerogative, or, as by Cromwell, to urge parliament not to claim too much, but to co-operate with him in his task of government. Here we see the early stages of a new idea, that members of parliament were bound, as trustees, to carry out the expressed wishes of their constituents. This opens up the whole question of the position of M.P.s as representatives, free to use their discretion, or as mere delegates or mouthpieces of the will of the electorate. Into this, however, or into the associated idea that legislation should only be undertaken by parliament if it has the backing of a 'mandate' from the people, I have no space to enter here.[2]

Another form of parliamentary trusteeship appears in Richard Baxter's *A Holy Commonwealth*. He ascribes the establishment of monarchy to a contract, explicit or implicit, between prince and people, in which the people reserved certain rights for themselves, over which the prince was to have no power. Parliament, according to Baxter, 'representeth the people as free', but, he proceeded to explain, what he meant by this was that the people under government were not wholly free, but only

[1] Quoted in C. S. Emden, *The People and the Constitution* (Oxford, 1933), p. 317; cf. ibid., p. 14.
[2] See ibid., on the whole question of the popular mandate.

free in respect of these rights that they had retained and exempted from the prince's power. Parliament, he declared, 'are their Trustees for the securing of those exempted rights'. Members of parliament are not conceived here as trustees for the securing of any particular interest of individual constituencies, but rather as charged with the duty of seeing that the contract between king and people is not broken.[1]

A more ordinary use of the trust concept is that in Dryden's 'Epistle to the Whigs' at the beginning of *The Medal*,[2] where he tells them that they are not 'the trustees of the public liberty'; or when Halifax, in his celebrated pamphlet, *The Anatomy of an Equivalent*, refers to countries 'where the supreme assemblies are not constant standing courts, but called together upon occasions, and composed of such as the People chuse for that time only, with a Trust and character that remaineth no longer with them than till that assembly is regularly dissolved'.[3]

We can see, then, that whether applied to executive or to legislature, the trust concept reached Locke in a well-developed form, and that he did no more than receive and apply it. After the Revolution there was little further reason for insistence on the duties of the king as a trustee. An occasional controversy might resuscitate the idea, but as far as the powers of the king were concerned, Locke only stated finally what was already secured by the development of the constitution. When Bolingbroke later declared that the patriot king 'will make one, and but one, distinction between his rights and those of his people: he will look on his to be a trust, and theirs a property. He will discern

[1] R. Baxter, *A Holy Commonwealth* (1659), p. 458.

[2] Par. 2.

[3] p. 10. Cf. also his remarks on obligations (p. 15): 'The obligation is yet more binding when the Trust is of a Public nature . . . perhaps no crime of any kind can outdo such a deliberate breach of Trust.'

that he can have a right to no more than is trusted to him by the constitution',[1] he was stating a principle that no eighteenth-century king of England would have thought of questioning.

In its parliamentary form, however, the trust concept had an important future before it in the eighteenth century, and figured prominently not only on particular occasions of dispute but in general political writings. Parliament's treatment of the Kentish petitioners, for example, aroused a bitter party controversy, in which Whig pamphleteers hastened to chastise their Tory opponents, pointing out that the Commons 'ought to be, what they reckon themselves, *Trustees* and *Guardians* of the Liberties of England', and that it was tyranny 'when a few who are chosen to be Trustees and Guardians of the people's liberties bring the people under their absolute power'.[2] Then again, the peers who protested against the Septennial Act (1716) urged that it deprived the people 'of the only remedy which they have against those, who either do not understand, or through corruption do wilfully betray the trust reposed in them; which remedy is, to choose better men in their places'.[3] Bolingbroke, who largely followed Locke's principles, maintained that 'parliaments are the true guardians of liberty. For this

[1] *The Idea of a Patriot King* (1738), in *Works* (1809 edn.), iv. 262. A slight variation, with a note of reciprocity which makes it approach the contract theory, appears in Bolingbroke's *Dissertation on Parties* (1733–4), Letter xiv: 'The king, when he commands, discharges a trust, and performs a duty, as well as the subject, when he obeys.'

[2] Lord Somers, *Jura Populi Anglicani* . . . (1701), pp. 28, 29. The source of inspiration here was undoubtedly Locke, for he is mentioned and quoted on the next page. Further reference to the trust concept may be found on pp. 50, 51, and 53.

[3] Grant Robertson, p. 202. Another aspect of the idea of the trusteeship of parliament appears at the time of the Wilkes controversy (1763) in the dissentient resolution in the Lords against concurrence with the Commons in limiting the scope of parliamentary privilege (ibid., p. 449).

principally they were instituted; and this is the principal article of that great and noble Trust which the collective body of the people of Britain reposes in their representative'.[1]

By this time, one might think, the political trust would always take the form of an unmistakably legal metaphor. But investigation shows that it was often so vaguely expressed as to suggest that it was still associated, as in the earlier stages of its development, as much with the general sense of trust as with the equitable trust proper. On the one hand, there is a legal metaphor when the electors of Sussex tell their M.P.s that they will not 'instruct or direct you our representative how to discharge that high trust which we by our choice have called you to';[2] but when we find that in the same year (1701) Somers advised the king to change his ministers, because 'to set himself and his people at ease, he must trust those whom the body of the people do not distrust',[3] the meaning seems to be quite general. So again, when Junius charged parliament with betraying its trust,[4] or when Richard Price referred to the House of Commons as 'the persons to whom the trust of government is committed', and said that 'they possess no power beyond the limits of the trust for the execution of which they were formed',[5] or when the Whig candidates for the county of Norfolk at the election of 1784 stated that

[1] *Dissertation on Parties*, Letter x. In Letter xi he insists on the necessity of frequent elections so that 'the people should have frequent opportunities of calling their representatives to account, as it were, for the discharge of the trust committed to them'. There are numerous further references, in this letter and in Letter xiii, to M.P.s being trustees chosen by the electorate. In Letter xiii he also (inconsistently) alludes to 'a bargain, a conditional contract', between 'the representative and collective bodies of the nation'.

[2] Emden, p. 18.   [3] Ibid., p. 173.

[4] Junius, *Letters*, xxxvii (1772 edn. ii. 74).

[5] *Observations on Civil Liberty* (1776), quoted in H. W. C. Davis, *The Age of Grey and Peel* (Oxford, 1929), p. 55.

it would be their 'mutual determination to discharge the important trust reposed in us with fidelity and independence',[1] we clearly seem to be dealing with a legal metaphor. When, on the other hand, we read a petition from the county of Somerset (1769) praying the king to dissolve parliament because 'your people can no longer place a confidence' in it,[2] or find Fox in a speech on a motion of Grey's for reform, in 1797, complaining that 'when we contend that ministers have not the confidence of the people, they tell us that parliament is the faithful representative of the sense of the country', and alluding to the people having 'an opportunity of choosing faithful organs of their opinion',[3] we can no longer say with such certainty that these are examples of the political trust, though they contain ideas that are akin to it. There were, in fact, two schools of thought in the eighteenth century on the position and duties of M.P.s.[4] Those who regarded them as delegates would be more apt to view their relationship with the electorate as being of the nature of an equitable trust, while others would be content with saying in a more general way that M.P.s must possess the trust or confidence of their constituents.

It is worth observing that the idea of the trusteeship of parliament was strongly supported by the jurist Austin. After remarking that 'the King and the Lords, with the members of the Commons' house, form a tripartite body

[1] Emden, p. 183. Cf. also p. 29, when Canning told his constituents at Liverpool at the election of 1812 that if he found that he came to disagree with them on any important point, 'I will not abuse my trust, but will give you the earliest opportunity of recalling or reconsidering your delegation of it'.

[2] Ibid., p. 185.

[3] Ibid., p. 194. Cf. also such a commonly used phrase as that a minister must 'possess the confidence' of parliament or of the people.

[4] Burke's relations with his constituents at Bristol form the classical instance of a dispute over this point.

which is sovereign and supreme', Austin proceeds to correct this by the statement that 'speaking accurately, the members of the Commons' house are merely trustees for the body by which they are elected and appointed: and, consequently, the sovereignty always resides in the King and the Peers, with the electoral body of the Commons. That a trust is imposed by the party delegating, and that the party representing engages to discharge the trust, seems to be imported by the correlative expressions *delegation* and *representation*. It were absurd to suppose that the delegating empowers the representative party to defeat or abandon any of the purposes for which the latter is appointed.'[1]

Dicey takes Austin to task for this language, and points out that 'nothing is more certain than that no English judge ever conceded, or, under the present constitution, can concede, that Parliament is in any legal sense a "trustee" for the electors. Of such a feigned "trust" the courts know nothing', and the truth is that in law parliament is the sovereign power in the state. Austin, in fact, was confusing, or rather, failed to distinguish, the strict legal sovereignty of parliament, and the political sovereignty of the electorate. But though legally sovereign, there are limits in practice to what parliament can do, and this limitation he expressed 'not very happily' by the idea that M.P.s were subject to a trust imposed by the electorate.[2]

---

[1] J. Austin, *Jurisprudence* (5th edn., 1885), i. 246.

[2] A. V. Dicey, *The Law of the Constitution* (10th edn.), pp. 75, 76. On similar grounds Dicey also criticizes the protest of the peers against the Septennial Act, whereas 'that act proves to demonstration that in a legal point of view Parliament is neither the agent of the electors nor in any sense a trustee for its constituents' (pp. 47–8). Actually Austin admitted (p. 247) that 'the trust imposed by the electoral body upon the body representing them in parliament is tacit rather than express: it arises from the relation between the bodies as delegating and representative parties, rather than from oral or written instructions', and therefore it is 'general and vague'

Legally, of course, Dicey is right. No court could entertain an action for breach of trust brought by an elector against an M.P. who had broken his so-called 'election pledges', any more than a court would enforce an attempt by a body of constituents to bind their member contractually to act according to their directions.[1] But to confine ourselves to strict matter of law does not dispose of the political trust. Austin was indeed guilty of confusion in his remark that 'speaking *accurately*' the Commons were trustees for the electorate; but if we recognize that the political trust is only metaphorically a trust, it may be a convenient way of stating that M.P.s, or other holders of power, are under an obligation (a moral obligation admittedly, not a legal obligation) to discharge certain duties. In the seventeenth century, when the principle of legal sovereignty was obscured by belief in fundamental law, it was possible to argue that this was actually a legal obligation. Our constitution has developed since then, and a modern government possesses a sovereignty far more absolute than any Stuart could have dreamed of, and intolerable if it were not exercised with a due sense of responsibility. Unless we are prepared to say that there are no real responsibilities or obligations in politics except strictly legal obligations, we cannot quarrel with the political trust concept on the ground that legally such a trust does not exist. The social contract theory has similarly been criticized on the ground that legally such a contract is imaginary. Now it seems to me that as political concepts the trust and the contract are fundamentally on much the same footing. They are both really metaphors, and rest

and 'simply enforced by moral sanctions'. As Dicey pointed out (p. 75, n. 2), this admission is 'fatal to the contention that Parliament is not in strictness a sovereign', and it really serves to show that the trust is only a metaphor.

[1] Cf. Emden, pp. 27, 28: he quotes Lord Loreburn's judgement in the Osborne case (1909).

on a resemblance, or an analogy, which is admittedly not an identity, between the political relationships they describe and the legal relationships of trust and contract proper.[1] There are further objections to the contract theory as an explanation of political obligation, which I need not enlarge on here, but to them the idea of political trusteeship is not open,[2] with the result that as it has played, so, properly understood, it still plays a useful part in political thought.

Like the equitable trust itself, it is both in origin and development a peculiarly English idea. Though there is indeed a superficial similarity between an English trust or 'use' and the *fideicommissum* or *ususfructus* of Roman law, the development of English equity followed peculiarly English lines, while the legal institutions of continental Europe were far more influenced by the ideas and phraseology of Roman law, and it seems to be agreed that the English trust does not owe its origin to any Roman institution. One result of this in the political sphere has been that whereas the thought of continental thinkers was often forced into contractual terms, English thinkers had in the trust concept a fruitful alternative to the idea of contract. We have seen that in practice they sometimes confused the two, but there is no need for us to do so, and since a trust in English law is something quite distinct from a contract, the trust concept in politics should also be kept distinct from any form of the social contract, even though it may sometimes (but not necessarily) be a way of expressing a similar idea.

To say that the trust concept is free from some of the

---

[1] Cf. my *Social Contract* (Oxford, 2nd edn. corrected, 1963), pp. 5, 6, 245.

[2] In particular, it need have no association with a 'state of nature', or an 'individualist' theory of government by consent, even if so associated in Locke.

defects of the social contract is not necessarily to approve
of all the uses to which it has been put. But while I have no
space to discuss these here,[1] before concluding I must
mention briefly the most recent field in which the trust
concept has found employment. Since Burke first referred
to the British government of India in terms of trusteeship,[2]
the trust concept was more and more freely applied to
colonial affairs, until in 1919 it came to be embodied in the
Covenant of the League of Nations. Article 22 provided
for the application of the principle that the 'well-being and
development' of peoples 'not yet able to stand by themselves under the strenuous conditions of the modern world

[1] One example which may be mentioned briefly is the frequent use of the
trust concept in the nineteenth century as an argument against the secret
ballot. J. S. Mill, for instance, disagreed with 'Mr. Bright and his school of
democrats', who held that 'the franchise is what they term a right, not
a trust'. 'The exercise of any political function', according to Mill, 'either
as an elector or as a representative, is power over others.' But, he maintained,
'in whatever way we define or understand the idea of a right, no person can
have a right (except in the purely legal sense) to power over others: every
such power . . . is morally, in the fullest force of the term, a trust' (J. S. Mill,
Representative Government (1861), c. x). Palmerston and others held similar
views: cf. E. L. Woodward, *The Age of Reform* (Oxford, 1938), pp. 86, 162.
What Mill, who here seems to be echoing Burke (cf. the next note), really
means is clearly not that the franchise is literally a legal trust, but that
political power involves a real moral obligation, of a kind analogous to the
duty of trusteeship in the sphere of law.

[2] Cf. Burke's 'Speech on Mr. Fox's East India Bill' (1783), in *Works* (1826
edn.,), iv. 11, in which he described 'every species of political dominion and
. . . commercial privilege' as 'in the strictest sense a trust; and it is of the
essence of every trust to be rendered accountable; and even totally to cease,
when it substantially varies from the purposes for which alone it can have
a lawful existence'. Burke seems to have thought naturally of moral obligation in terms of trusteeship: cf. his remark that the rich are 'trustees for
those who labour' (*Thoughts on Scarcity*, quoted in H. J. Laski, *The Rise of
European Liberalism* (1936), p. 200). It is interesting to observe that as the
self-governing colonies grew to the status of dominions they became anxious
to throw off the theory of trusteeship. Cf. Sir Robert Borden's remarks at
the Imperial War Conference in 1917, quoted in A. B. Keith, *Selected Speeches
and Documents on British Colonial Policy, 1763–1917*, ii. 377–8.

... form a sacred trust of civilisation, and that securities for the performance of this trust should be embodied in this Covenant. The best method', it proceeded, 'of giving practical effect to this principle is that the tutelage of such peoples should be entrusted to advanced nations . . . and that this tutelage should be exercised by them as Mandatories on behalf of the League.'

Maitland called the political trust a metaphor, and rightly so. But in this latest guide it was given a status of actuality in the sphere of international if not of municipal law, since the mandatory powers had a responsibility to the League, through its permanent Mandates Commission, to which they were to present annual reports on the conduct of their mandates. This mandatory trusteeship under the Covenant might be criticized as being merely a hypocritical cloak for imperialist exploitation, or as meaningless in practice, because the authority of the League of Nations was proved by experience to be ineffectual. Such criticisms, however, are not free from prejudice, and in any case they do not affect the fact that in principle the Covenant embodied a new juridical status in international law,[1] which was continued (and under its own name, too)

[1] On this see, for instance, R. Coupland, *The American Revolution and the British Empire* (1930), c. vi, especially pp. 193, 201, 209, and his *The Empire in These Days* (1935), pp. 164, 165, and c. xiii. See also C. M. MacInnes, *The British Commonwealth and its Unsolved Problems* (1925), c. iv. Other references for the principle of colonial trusteeship are given in the footnote to Maitland, *Selected Essays* (Cambridge, 1936), p. 221. The classical exposition of the principle is, of course, in F. D. Lugard, *The Dual Mandate in British Tropical Africa* (2nd edn., 1923). See also a lecture by D. Campbell Lee, *The Mandate for Mesopotamia and the Principle of Trusteeship in English Law* (1921). He suggested (pp. 9 ff.) that the word mandate was an unfortunate one to describe territory governed under Article 22 of the Covenant. It was chosen, no doubt, because of its use in continental countries whose institutions are largely influenced by Roman law, in which it is the regular technical term for a contract of agency. But, as he pointed out, the principle involved in Article 22 was really derived not from the Roman-law contract of *mandatum*

by the Trusteeship Council in the new organization of
the United Nations.

at all, but was entirely the product of the English idea of the trust, which
had come to permeate British colonial policy since the time of Burke.

The adjective *sacred*, often applied to the colonial trust, was presumably
meant to indicate that the obligation involved was not strictly legal but
moral, or rather religious.

VIII

THE DEVELOPMENT OF LOCKE'S
BELIEF IN TOLERATION

LOCKE's famous *Letter concerning Toleration* was not published till 1689, not long before the *Two Treatises of Government* and the *Essay concerning Human Understanding*, but the question of toleration had been occupying his mind for many years before this. In the *Treatises*, in which he incorporated the doctrines which had been advocated for a generation and more by a whole school of political writers, he summed up the Whig support for constitutionalism and opposition to arbitrary government. So also his belief in toleration, which was based on the same general principles as his political theory, was the fruit of long reading and reflection on a question of burning topical interest. In England, the intolerance of the Laudian Church, and later of the Presbyterians in the Long Parliament, had led the protestant sectaries to urge the necessity for religious liberty. Across the Atlantic the intolerant Calvinism of Massachusetts had aroused a similar controversy, which can be paralleled by the struggle for recognition by the Arminians in Holland and the Huguenots in France. With many of the sectaries the plea for toleration had been the outcome of their circumstances: they found themselves in the position of a persecuted minority, and had they been numerous enough to impose their beliefs on others some of them might have been as intolerant as their persecutors. But there were others whose belief in religious liberty was more profound than

this. Such was Oliver Cromwell himself, under whose protectorate some measure of toleration, for the protestant
sects if not for Roman Catholics or Anglicans, had actually
been secured for a time. Such also was Dr. John Owen, the
Independent divine who was Dean of Christ Church while
Locke was an undergraduate there.

After all, if toleration in the end was necessitated in
practice by the multiplicity and variety of the sects, religious liberty was logically the outcome of the protestant
belief that each individual (with God's assistance) could
interpret scripture for himself. To the rational spirit
which became more widespread as the seventeenth century advanced, an intolerant dogmatism seemed out of
place, and began to give way before the latitudinarian idea
that essential Christianity could be reduced to a few fundamental beliefs, compared with which all other matters,
whether of doctrine or ritual, were relatively unimportant.
Alongside this there appeared the idea of 'natural religion',
which subsequently reached its fullest development among
the Deists, but which had much earlier roots. Just as
natural law, which was God's will for human conduct,
could be discerned by the faculty of reason, so, it was
thought, the principles of religion, with which morality
was closely connected, were founded in nature and could
be discerned, independently of revelation or of ecclesiastical authority, by natural reason. Those who thought
thus would be inclined to regard many of the subjects in
dispute between the different churches as inessential
trivialities. To many minds, also, the rationalism of the
age meant a more purely secular outlook, which was
sceptical of ecclesiastical dogma, and more inclined to be
influenced by practical than by theological considerations.
Dissent was strong among the mercantile classes, and they
were not slow to argue that English traders suffered in

comparison with the Dutch, whose prosperity they ascribed to the religious liberty allowed in Holland. Writers like Shaftesbury, Temple, Petty, and others stressed these arguments, and it can hardly be doubted that this appeal to material interest contributed powerfully to reinforce the more purely intellectual grounds in favour of toleration.[1]

Locke, who was the son of Puritan parents, whose education both at Westminster and at Oxford had been in a Puritan atmosphere, and who subsequently became closely associated with the sceptical and tolerant Shaftesbury, was in fundamental sympathy with this rationalist point of view.[2] In politics the attitude he adopted, in common with the Whigs, was one of resistance to the dogmatic authoritarianism professed by the Tories with the support of the established church. Instead of their conception of church and state as so integrally linked together in one divinely organized society that membership of the one essentially involved membership of the other, he regarded the state as a voluntary union of individuals for the specific and limited purposes of settling disputes, preserving order, and protecting life and property. Corresponding with this was his view of a church as, similarly, a voluntary union of individuals for specific purposes, namely, 'the public worship of God in such manner as they believe will be acceptable to the Deity for the salvation of their souls'.[3]

[1] See A. A. Seaton, *The Theory of Toleration under the Later Stuarts* (Cambridge, 1911), cc. 2 and 3.

[2] According to Burnet (*Own Time*, ii. c. 1; ed. Airy, i. 172), Shaftesbury was 'a Deist at best'. Though brought up in Puritan surroundings, Locke was never a Puritan himself. He supported the rights of dissenters, but his real affinity was with the liberal school of divines to which Cudworth and Tillotson, Patrick and Isaac Barrow belonged (cf. Fox Bourne, *Life of John Locke*, i. 310).

[3] *A Letter on Toleration* (ed. Klibansky and Gough (Oxford, 1968)), p. 71. See also Locke's paper, dated 1673–4, 'On the difference between civil and

This being so, each society will have its own laws and conditions of membership, but neither has any right to interfere in the affairs of the other for purposes which are purely the other's concern. Thus it is the state's business to keep the peace, but it is none of the state's business to impose civil penalties in order to enforce obedience to the laws of the church. The proper method of enforcing such obedience is the hope of rewards and fear of punishments in the other world, except that, as the church has to maintain its existence in this world, it may expel members who do not accept its principles or obey its regulations. Here we see the essential points round which Locke's advocacy of toleration always centred.

That his conern with this subject dated back to 1660 has been known since Lord King printed part of the preface to a then unpublished treatise of that date, entitled *Question: Whether the Civil Magistrate may lawfully impose and determine the use of indifferent things in reference to Religious Worship*.[1] Investigation of the Lovelace Collection of Locke's papers has revealed a good deal more than Lord King disclosed about this treatise, and has also shown that Locke's attitude to toleration was already defined in 1659. This appears from a letter to one S. H., thanking him for a book he had sent on toleration, which Locke declares that he has

ecclesiastical power', endorsed 'Excommunication', among the Lovelace papers, and printed in Lord King, *Life of John Locke* (Bohn's edn.), p. 300. In this he works out in parallel columns the comparison between 'Civil Society or the State' and 'Religious Society or the Church', an arrangement which emphasizes his fundamental concept of both church and state as associations of individuals. Actually he describes churches as more voluntary than states, for while mankind 'are combined into civil societies in various forms, as force, chance, agreement or other accidents have happened to constrain them', and governments once established can command their subjects' continued obedience, 'church membership is perfectly voluntary, and may end whenever anyone pleases without any prejudice to himself' (ibid., p. 304).

[1] King, op. cit., p. 7.

read with great pleasure and admiration. He hopes there will be a second and enlarged edition, and to this end he gives advice on how to make the book more effective polemically, suggesting that the author could improve it by tracing the history of toleration down to recent times and dealing with conditions in Holland, France, and Poland. Locke's doubt was whether S. H. was wise in advocating a general toleration for all, including Roman Catholics, and he gave reasons for thinking such wide indulgence dangerous.[1] Dr. W. von Leyden, who calendared the Lovelace papers in the Bodleian Library, identified S. H. with Henry Stubbe (it was apparently Locke's habit, when denoting someone by his initials, to reverse their order), who was a friend of Hobbes and had been a contemporary of Locke's at Westminster and Christ Church. The book in question, published in 1659, must have been Stubbe's *An Essay in Defence of the Good Old Cause; or a Discourse concerning the Rise and Extent of the Power of the Civil Magistrate in Reference to Spiritual Affairs . . .*, in the course of which the writer claimed to vindicate Sir Henry Vane from the 'false aspersions of Mr. Baxter'. Locke never ceased to think it unsafe to extend toleration to Roman Catholics (whom in this respect he bracketed with atheists), because Roman Catholics not only taught that faith need not be kept with heretics, but owed allegiance to a foreign potentate who pretended that kings forfeited their crowns if he excommunicated them.

For Locke the essential question was thus a political one. It was not a question of freedom of conscience, or of intellectual freedom, in the abstract. It was a question of the extent of the power of the civil magistrate in religious affairs. In civil affairs, as we have seen,[2] Locke held that

[1] Draft of the letter in Bodl. MS. Locke c. 27, f. 1.
[2] Above, p. 119.

civil magistrates and governments had absolute power, but in religious affairs they could interfere only in so far as such interference was necessary for civil purposes, such as the preservation of peace, and did not go beyond matters 'indifferent'. This was the line he took in the treatise he composed in 1660, in reply to a pamphlet published anonymously in that year with the title, *The Great Question concerning Things Indifferent in Religious Worship Briefly Stated*. Dr. von Leyden has shown that the author of this was another old Westminster, Edward Bagshaw (the younger), who, like Locke, also became a student of Christ Church. Bagshaw championed the extreme sectarian view that the civil magistrate could never interfere in any religious matters; but Locke, while agreeing that the magistrate had no power to touch things necessary for the worship of God, and determined and revealed by God as such, argued that indifferent things are subject to the magistrate's interference, since the way they are determined is not necessary for the maintenance of religion, but may affect questions of peace and order. The Lovelace Collection contains a copy of Bagshaw's pamphlet; and each of Locke's arguments in the treatise, which consists of thirty-six quarto sheets, is introduced by a quotation from Bagshaw, to which it is a reply.[1] Locke discussed his controversy with Bagshaw with other Oxford friends, as appears from letters to him from Samuel Tilly, and Gabriel Towerson of All Souls, while a couple of pages at the end of the treatise

[1] Bodl. MS. Locke e. 7. It is possible, as Lord King suggested, that Locke refrained from publication when the scheme of comprehension with the Presbyterians broke down, and it became clear that the post-Restoration parliament was determined to impose a policy of Anglican uniformity. Locke, who disliked public controversy, may well have felt that in these circumstances there would be no point in publishing his treatise. Cf. P. Abrams (ed.), John Locke, *Two Tracts on Government* (Cambridge, 1967), pp. 12–15.

contain a draft of a letter from him, dated Pensford,[1] 11
December 1660, and signed 'John Locke', which Dr. von
Leyden thinks was probably addressed to Towerson, who
seems to have instigated him to write the treatise. It looks
as if Locke intended to publish it, possibly anonymously
like Bagshaw's pamphlet itself, but he never did so, and
with characteristic caution he subsequently crossed out the
draft letter and tried (not quite successfully) to make both
his signature and the word 'Pensford' illegible. The letter to
Towerson summarizes the contents of the treatise, and contains a number of sentences which also occur at the end of
the Preface to the Reader. The passages printed by Lord
King consist only of some excerpts from this Preface,
which is written in Locke's hand on six sides of a sheet of
paper, originally folded and now bound separately from
the treatise itself.[2]

From this it seems clear that, in his disgust at the
fanatical excesses of the Interregnum, Locke not only at
first welcomed the Restoration, but was prepared to attribute a greater authority to the government than he thought
proper in later years. After declaring that 'there is no one
can have a greater respect and veneration for authority
than I', he remarks that from earliest childhood he has
found himself 'in a storm, which has lasted almost
hitherto', so that he 'cannot but entertain the approaches
of a calm with the greatest joy and satisfaction', and he
feels bound, therefore, 'both in duty and gratitude to endeavour the continuance of such a blessing by disposing
men's minds to obedience to that government which has

[1] Locke's home in north Somerset, where he was staying with his parents
at this time. See Abrams, op. cit., p. 11.

[2] Bodl. MS. Locke c. 28, ff. 1–2. The full texts of Locke's writings on
this occasion, with an Introduction discussing in detail the circumstances
that led to his composing them, have been published by Dr. P. Abrams, op.
cit.

brought with it the quiet settlement which even our giddy folly had put beyond the reach not only of our contrivance but hopes'. His wish is that men will not 'hazard again the substantial blessings of peace and settlement in an over-zealous contention about things which they themselves confess to be little, and at most are but indifferent'. Experience, he continues, has taught him that 'a general freedom is but a general bondage', and 'were the part of freedom contended for by our author [sc. Bagshaw] gener-ally indulged in England, it would prove only a liberty for contention, censure and persecution'. He is no believer, therefore, in 'a liberty for ambitious men to pull down well-framed constitutions, that out of the ruins they may build themselves fortunes', or 'a liberty to be Christians so as not to be subjects. All the freedom I can wish my country or myself, is to enjoy the protection of those laws which the prudence and providence of our ancestors estab-lished, and the happy return of His Majesty has restored.' As we have seen in previous studies, in the political theory of his maturity Locke upheld the traditional English constitution based on a limited monarchy and funda-mental law, but in this Preface he gave expression to markedly less 'liberal' views.

Locke opens the treatise itself by laying down certain propositions, which are of considerable interest, as showing that at this early date he had already formulated some of the basic principles of his political theory, and they are therefore worth quoting:

In order to the clearer debating this question, besides the granting my author's two suppositions, viz.: (i) That a Chris-tian may be a magistrate, (ii) that there are some things in-different, it will not be amiss to premiss some few things about these matters of indifferency, viz.:

  1. That were there no law there would be no moral good or

evil, but man would be left to a most entire liberty in all his actions, and could meet with nothing which would not be purely indifferent, and consequently, that which doth not lie under the obligation of any law is still indifferent.

2. That nobody hath a natural original power and disposure of this liberty of man but only God himself, from whose authority all laws do fundamentally derive their obligation, as being either immediately enjoined by him, or framed by some authority derived from him.

3. That wherever God hath made known his will, either by the discovery of reason, usually called the law of nature, or the revelations of his word, there nothing is left man but submission and obedience, and all things within the compass of this law are necessarily and indispensably good or evil.

4. That all things not comprehended in that law are perfectly indifferent, and as to them man is naturally free, but yet so much master of his own liberty that he may by compact convey it over to another, and invest him with a power over his actions, there being no law of God forbidding a man to dispose of his liberty and obey another. But on the other side, there being a law of God enforcing fidelity and truth in all lawful contracts, it obliges him after such resignation and agreement to submit.

Locke's fifth proposition, quoted above,[1] emphasizes the necessity, if life in society is to be possible, for 'every particular man' to 'part with this right to his liberty'[2] and entrust the government with supreme power.

Indifferency and the powers of the magistrate were being debated at length in numerous publications about this time, and at Christ Church, which in the course of the year 1660 was presided over by no less than four Deans of varying outlook and policy in these matters, such

[1] p. 119.
[2] Locke first of all wrote 'native right' and 'primitive liberty', but crossed out the adjectives.

indifferent things as the wearing of surplices were in utter disorder.[1] It was against this background that Locke rejected Bagshaw's plea for religious liberty. Bagshaw rested his claim for complete freedom, in everything not expressly commanded or forbidden in Scripture, on faith and revelation, but Locke argued that natural law and reason made it evident that only limited toleration was consistent with life in society. He agreed that right and wrong were determined by the law of nature or the will of God, but indifferent things must be subject to the civil magistrate, since he was responsible for the maintenance of public order.

Locke's attitude in 1660 thus appears to be definitely conservative, but at the same time he maintained that his doctrine did not involve any damaging loss of liberty. 'Besides the submission I have for authority,' he wrote, 'I have no less a love of liberty, without which a man shall find himself less happy than a beast, slavery being a condition that robs us of all the benefits of life, and embitters the greatest blessings. . . .'[2] Locke also argued that 'if the supreme authority be conferred on the magistrate by the consent of the people, . . . then it is evident that they have resigned up their liberty of action into his disposure, and so all his commands are but their own votes, and his edicts their own injunctions made by proxies which by mutual contract they are bound to obey'.[3]

This and other passages are worth attention for the indication they give of what Locke meant by consent. It seems remarkable, to say the least, that he should recognize the impotence of the individual's vote in face of an adverse majority,[4] and at the same time conclude the

[1] Abrams, op. cit., pp. 30 ff.
[2] Preface to the Reader, printed in Abrams, op. cit., p. 120.
[3] Abrams, op. cit., p. 126.   [4] Cf. above, p. 119.

Preface to this treatise by remarking that 'it would be a strange thing if anyone amongst us should question the obligation of those laws which are not ratified nor imposed on him but *by his own consent* [my italics] in Parliament'. It seems probable that he thought of this consent as embodied in the contract by which, it was supposed, every man surrendered his own individual liberty of action at the origin of the state; and in a previous study we have already noticed the unconvincing arguments by which he sought to show that the same consent could be ascribed to later generations. The best explanation I can offer of Locke's apparent satisfaction with this is that the notion of consent in parliament had become such a commonplace of the constitution that when he was not paying special attention to what representation really involved (and sometimes even when he was) he was apt to give it the same everyday uncritical acceptance as the rest of his fellow countrymen seem to have done, then as well as since.

Besides the treatise in reply to Bagshaw, Locke also composed a short Latin treatise on the same subject, entitled *An Magistratus Civilis possit res adiaphoras in divini cultus ritus asciscere, eosque populo imponere? Aff.*[1] This differs in form and substance from the English treatise.[2] It makes no mention of Bagshaw's pamphlet, but after some definitions of 'magistrate', 'religious worship', and 'indifferent things', with discussions about the nature of law and the duty of civil obedience, deals more generally, and in a more scholastic manner, with the question of the rights of

---

[1] This consists of eighteen manuscript pages in Locke's handwriting (Bodl. MS. Locke c. 28, ff. 3–20). Another draft of it, in Locke's handwriting, will be found in the note-book entitled *Lemmata* (Bodl. MS. Locke e. 6), which also contains drafts of six of his Latin essays on the law of nature. The similarity to them in the form of the title will be observed.

[2] Latin text and an English translation in Abrams, op. cit., pp. 185 ff., 210 ff.

magistrates. Locke purported to preserve liberty of conscience, but he defined it in a very narrow way, arguing
that if the magistrate gave orders concerning things indifferent, a man must obey them, but as he need not
inwardly assent, his judgement remained free. We may
doubt the value of a liberty to think without the liberty
to act on one's thoughts, and in later life Locke ceased to
argue in this style, and came to hold that in religion there
were no indifferent things; but he continued to maintain
that the civil magistrate could always demand full
obedience when this was necessary for peace and security.
In view of Locke's numerous quotations from Hooker in
the *Second Treatise of Government*, it is interesting to observe
that in both the English and the Latin treatises on the civil
magistrate he cites Hooker in support of his view.[1] In the
English treatise Hooker's name is coupled with that of Dr.
Sanderson, while the first draft of the Latin treatise refers
to the Bishop of Lincoln, and Dr. von Leyden concluded
that the Latin treatise was written not before the autumn
of 1660, for Robert Sanderson, who had been Regius
Professor of Divinity at Oxford, was consecrated Bishop
of Lincoln on 28 October in that year. Locke cancelled the
reference to the bishop in his final draft of the Latin
treatise, although in fact his argument owed more to
Sanderson than to Hooker.[2]

In his *Life of John Locke* (1876) Fox Bourne quoted[3]
some extracts from a work, consisting of forty-six pages of
manuscript, said to be in Locke's hand, and preserved

[1] In the English treatise he is 'the learned and reverend Mr. Hooker',
in the Latin 'doctissimus Hooker'. The epithet 'judicious', which appeared
on the title-page of a series of extracts from Hooker published in 1675, was,
according to the *O.E.D.*, first applied to him in 1626, in Thomas Jackson's
commentary on the Creed.

[2] His reasons for so doing are discussed by Abrams, op. cit., pp. 70 ff.

[3] Fox Bourne, op. cit., i. 147 ff.

among the Shaftesbury papers in the Public Record Office, entitled *Reflections upon the Roman Commonwealth*. This is not dated, but Fox Bourne thought it belonged to the year 1660, and might have been written before the treatise on the civil magistrate which we have just dealt with. It shows considerable knowledge of Roman history and historians, and political convictions from which Locke 'never greatly swerved'. The constitution is, perhaps, chiefly remarkable for the liberality of the religious institutions, which, begun by Romulus and completed by Numa, are commended for their simplicity and wisdom. Some of the phraseology of this essay, together with its advocacy of 'comprehension', and the belief that the essentials of religion could be reduced to one or two simple articles, without 'clogging it with creeds and catechisms and endless niceties about the essences, properties and attributes of God', certainly seem to have a Lockian sound. On the other hand, these views were common to the Whigs and Latitudinarians in general, and the power the magistrate is here allowed to exercise in religious matters differs from what Locke elsewhere attributes to the civil authorities. Locke's favourite distinction was between things morally good or bad, which a man is obliged to do or to abstain from, and things 'indifferent', and it is in the latter that the magistrate might (in certain circumstances) intervene; but here the suggestion is that the lawgiver may 'venture to enjoin' belief in 'the common principles of religion' which 'all mankind agree in'. Internal evidence therefore makes it doubtful whether Locke was really the author of this essay at all. It has been attributed to the third Lord Shaftesbury, but it has been shown to be in fact the first part of Walter Moyle's *Essay upon the Roman Government*.[1]

[1] W. Moyle, *Works* (1726), i. 3. See H. F. Russell Smith, *Harrington and his Oceana* (Cambridge, 1914), pp. 139, 143, 217–18.

It is clear from entries in Locke's commonplace book, dated 1661,[1] that he gave a good deal of attention to questions about the nature of the church, and the power of the government in religious matters, and that he soon advanced from the position he had taken up in the treatise against Bagshaw. Under the heading *Sacerdos* he noted that 'though the magistrate have a power of commanding or forbidding things indifferent which have a relation to religion, yet this can only be within that Church whereof he himself is a member'. He may 'forbid such things as may tend to the disturbance of the peace of the commonwealth', whether people think them civil or religious; but he may not 'order and direct even matters indifferent in the circumstances of a worship, or within a Church whereof he is not professor or member'. Rites and ceremonies are 'a thing different and independent wholly from every man's concern in the civil society, which hath nothing to do with a man's affairs in the other world. . . .

[1] Dr. Abrams (op. cit., p. 9) doubts the existence of this book, but there undoubtedly exists a book, with the date of Locke's birth and the words 'Adversaria 1661' at the beginning, as described by Lord King (op. cit., p. 282). It is in America, in the private collection of Mr. Arthur Houghton, Jr., and a microfilm (MS. Film 77) is available for English readers in the Bodleian Library. One difficulty is that its present contents only partially correspond with the contents as described by King. Abrams says that the passages King quoted 'come from two separate notebooks' and are all plainly dated by Locke as entries made after 1680. King was not an impeccably accurate transcriber, but it seems to me at least doubtful that he should have been so careless as to have said that he was copying from one notebook what in fact he was copying from two. A possible explanation is that what was in King's time one book may have since been split up, and in the process pages may have been displaced. This is only a conjecture, but it would account for the curious fact that the entry marked *Sacerdos*, which King quoted as one continuous passage, is now in two discontinuous sections, with one of the versions of the 1667 *Essay concerning Toleration* between them. No doubt, while Locke started his Commonplace Book in 1661, some of the entries in it were made years later, and Abrams may well be right in his contention that there is nothing in Locke's papers before 1667 that shows support for religious toleration.

The magistrate hath here no more right to intermeddle than any private man.' This rather hesitant and illogical compromise was already an advance on 1660; but in 1689 Locke confines the magistrate's power to purely civil affairs; it 'extends not to the establishing of any articles of faith, or forms of worship, by the force of his laws', and the fact that a magistrate is a member of a particular church gives him no more power, as a magistrate, to interfere in its religious affairs than in the religious affairs of any other church.

Another entry, headed *Ecclesia*, develops Locke's position a little further. He finds support in Hooker for the notion that the church is a supernatural but voluntary society: voluntary, because, like other societies, the 'original of it' is 'an inclination unto sociable life and a consent to the bond of association which is the law and order they are associated in': supernatural, because 'part of the bond of their association is a law revealed concerning what worship God would have done unto him, which natural reason could not have discovered'. From these premisses Locke draws four conclusions: (1) the secular power 'which is purely natural' cannot compel anyone to belong to any one of the many existing churches, (2) nobody can 'impose any ceremonies unless positively and clearly by revelation injoined', (3) only the revealed part of the bond of association is an unalterable law; the other, being human, 'depends wholly on consent, and so is alterable, and a man is held by such laws, or to such a particular society, no longer than himself doth consent', (4) churches do not (as Hooker seems to imply) originate from our inclination to a sociable life, for this can be fully satisfied in other societies, but 'from the obligation man, by the light of reason, finds himself under, to own and worship God publicly in the world'.[1]

[1] Lord King, op. cit., pp. 286 ff., 295.

In these brief notes we can see already formed Locke's basic ideas on the voluntary character of societies, and of the church as one of them; and of the relationship in this connexion between God's will and man's natural reason. The theoretical structure of his political philosophy, of which his theory of toleration was a corollary, is already here in outline. It was confirmed and substantiated by further reading and reflection, and required only to be more fully worked out in the light of experience of practical affairs. This practical experience Locke gained meanwhile through his association with Shaftesbury, but it was not till after the publication of some of Filmer's works in 1679 that he determined to write at full length on the principles of government. In the intervening years, however, though he published nothing, his papers show that questions about the churches and toleration occupied a large part of his thoughts.

To this period belong *The Fundamental Constitutions for the Government of Carolina*, of which the original draft, in Locke's handwriting, dated 21 June 1669, is among the Shaftesbury papers in the Public Record Office. Charles II granted a charter for this colony to eight Lords Proprietors, among whom Ashley (later Lord Shaftesbury) was prominent, and Locke, who was in effect Ashley's confidential secretary, was closely concerned in the drafting of this scheme; and the text, as subsequently adopted by the Lords Proprietors, after being published in a volume entitled *A Collection of Several Pieces of Mr. John Locke* (1720), was included in later collected editions of Locke's *Works*. It seems to be generally agreed, however, that though Locke drafted this, the scheme itself was not his.[1] To students of his thought it is perhaps mainly of

[1] Locke's *Works* also contain a paper entitled *A Letter from a Person of Quality to his Friend in the Country*, which arose out of the proceedings in the

interest on account of the extremely liberal religious clauses it contains. In effect, colonists were to profess a belief in God, consent to worship him, and make no secret of their belief: with these provisos, any seven persons could establish a church of their own, and worship God in whatever manner they thought fit, so long as they did not interfere with a like freedom for others, or speak seditiously about the government. There was also a clause (which, we are told, 'was not drawn up by Mr. Locke, but inserted by some of the chief of the proprietors, against his judgement, as Mr. Locke himself informed one of his friends')[1] providing that when the colony was sufficiently developed Anglican churches should be established and these only should be subsidized by the government.

Shaftesbury himself believed in religious liberty, and even if Locke did no more than draft this constitution, the comprehensiveness of its religious arrangements and their freedom from any rigid tests are entirely in accord with his views. Fox Bourne suggested that 'whether Locke originated those generous arrangements or not, he was certainly responsible for the wording of them, in which the generosity was clearly expressed'. This is confirmed by some letters to Locke preserved in the Lovelace Collection, notably three letters on Carolina from Sir Peter Colleton, the second of which (undated, but endorsed '1673') refers to 'that excellent form of government in the composure of which you had so great a hand',[2] and a letter from Nicolas Toinard, dated 16 September 1679, in which the writer

Lords over a bill for imposing the so-called Bishops' Test (1675). Shaftesbury seems to have got Locke to write out an account of his opposition to this bill. This was privately printed, but it was ordered to be burned by the common hangman, and Locke denied the authorship of it. See Lord King, op. cit., p. 39, Fox Bourne, op. cit. i. 238 ff., 336; H. O. Christophersen, *A Bibliographical Introduction to the Study of John Locke* (Oslo, 1930), p. 9.

[1] Fox Bourne, op. cit., i. 240.   [2] Bodl. MS. Locke, c. 6, f. 213.

says he has heard that Locke has been revising the article on religion in the constitutions of Carolina.[1]

Two years before the Carolina scheme, Locke had completed the draft of what Fox Bourne called 'by far the most important of Locke's early writings'.[2] We have already noticed entries in his commonplace book on the subject of the church and religious worship. In 1667 he assembled his conclusions on this subject in an orderly form, under the heading *An Essay concerning Toleration*. It appears from the last sentence that he contemplated writing more on the same subject, but he does not seem to have done so. The Essay dates from the beginning of his acquaintance with Ashley, and it is possible that Ashley encouraged him to write it. Locke evidently took a great deal of trouble over the composition of this Essay, for four variant versions of it are in existence, the last of which, a copy in the handwriting of an amanuensis, contains a number of alterations, cancellations, and additional passages in Locke's own hand.[3] The version printed in Fox Bourne's *Life of John Locke*[4] was taken from a draft, in Locke's handwriting, among the Shaftesbury papers. The other two versions are both in America, one in the Huntington Library in California, the other in Locke's commonplace book in Mr. Houghton's private collection. Lord King[5] printed the end of this, with the concluding sentence 'sic cogitavit J. Locke' and the date (1667), with which Locke not infrequently ended the memoranda he made of his philosophical reflections.

In this Essay Locke makes clear at the outset that his

[1] Bodl. MS. Locke c. 20. The Constitutions are also referred to in a letter to Locke from H. Justel (MS. Locke c. 12).

[2] Fox Bourne, op. cit. i. 165.

[3] This final version is in Bodl. MS. Locke c. 28, ff. 21–32.

[4] Fox Bourne, op. cit., i. 174–94.

[5] Lord King, op. cit., p. 156.

theory of toleration is the logical consequence of his theory
of the nature of society and government. 'If men could live
peaceably and quietly together, without uniting under
certain laws, and entering[1] into a commonwealth, there
would be no need at all of magistrates or politics, which
were only made to preserve men in this world from the
fraud and violence of one another.' Whether the government be in the hands of a monarch *jure divino*, or of
magistrates deriving their authority 'from the grant and
consent of the people', the functions of a ruler are strictly
limited to 'securing the civil peace and property of his
subjects'. In reference to toleration, he continues, 'the
opinions and actions of men . . . divide themselves into
three sorts'. First, 'all purely speculative opinions and
divine worship', such as 'the belief of the Trinity, pur-
gatory, transubstantiation, antipodes,[2] Christ's personal
reign on earth, &c.,' and 'the place, time, and manner of
worshipping my God'. With these society and government
have no concern. Secondly, 'all practical opinions and
actions in matters of indifferency', which 'in their own
nature are neither good nor bad but yet concern society
and men's conversations with one another'. Thirdly, there
are 'moral virtues and vices', which 'concern society and
are also good or bad in their own nature'.

   Only the first of these have 'an absolute and universal
right to toleration'. In the second category Locke includes
'all practical principles or opinions, by which men think

   [1] 'entering' in the final version in the Lovelace Collection. The copy
printed by Fox Bourne read 'growing'. Locke's alteration is a significant
indication of his voluntarist theory of the nature of the state.
   [2] It must be remembered that in the seventeenth century the possibility
of antipodes was a theoretical and controversial question. It is worth
noticing that in the final version Locke added a passage making it clear that
the existence of God was not to be regarded as a speculative opinion, 'it
being the foundation of all morality', without which men would be like
wild beasts, 'incapable of all society'.

themselves obliged to regulate their actions with one
another; as that men may breed their children, or dispose
of their estates, as they please; that men may work or rest
when they think fit; that polygamy and divorce are lawful
or unlawful; that flesh or fish is to be eaten or abstained
from at certain seasons, and so on. These opinions, and
the actions following from them, with all other things indifferent, have a title also to toleration; but yet only so far
as they do not tend to the disturbance of the state, or do
not cause greater inconveniences than advantages to the
community.' The magistrate, therefore, 'may prohibit the
publishing of any of these opinions when in themselves[1]
they tend to the disturbance of the government', and may
command or forbid any actions resulting from these
opinions in so far as they affect 'the peace, safety and
security of his people'. But he must be careful to make no
laws and impose no restraints beyond what are so necessitated; nor should he force any man to renounce an
opinion or assent to the contrary, because such a compul-
sion 'cannot alter men's minds; it can only force them to
be hypocrites'. A similar principle applies to the third
category. 'However strange it may seem,' Locke declares,
'the law-maker hath nothing to do with moral virtues
and vices . . . any otherwise than barely as they are sub-
servient to the good and preservation of mankind under
government.' As a result, Locke thinks that while the
magistrate 'ought not to command the practice of any
vice', he is not bound to punish all vices, but may tolerate
some, 'for, I would know, what government in the world
doth not?' Locke briefly discusses the problem of men who
find the restrictions imposed by the magistrate conflict
with the 'sincere persuasions of their own consciences'. He
thinks such men should do what their consciences require

[1] 'in themselves' inserted in the final version in the Lovelace Collection.

of them, in so far as they can do so without violence, 'but withal are bound at the same time quietly to submit to the penalty the law inflicts on such disobedience. . . . And certainly he is a hypocrite, and only pretends conscience,' Locke declares, '. . . who will not, by obeying his conscience and submitting also to the law, purchase heaven for himself and peace for his country, though at the rate of his estate, liberty, or life itself.' We are apt to scoff nowadays at this doctrine of 'passive obedience', and it may indeed seem supine if applied indiscriminately, as it sometimes was by seventeenth-century high churchmen. But not everyone is heroic enough to resist actively, and even passive obedience may require considerable courage; and if the magistrate's interference is restricted by conditions such as Locke lays down, recalcitrants have no valid grounds for complaint.

Having dealt with toleration as a question of the magistrate's duty, Locke proceeds to discuss 'what he ought to do in prudence', with special reference to the papists and the 'fanatics'—an 'opprobrious name' for protestant dissenters, which he thinks should be 'laid aside and forgotten'. For the kind of reasons we have already noticed, he would exclude papists from toleration: besides, 'they think themselves bound to deny it to others'. As for the dissenters, if they cannot be persuaded to part with their opinions, it is useless to try and force them to do so by persecuting them. We may 'persuade them to lay by their animosities, and become friends to the state, though they are not sons of the church'.

In the earlier drafts of his Essay Locke expressed doubts whether it would be prudent for the government to tolerate all dissenting sects, especially if they 'herd themselves into companies with distinction from the public', and seem to the magistrate 'visibly to threaten the peace of

the state'. The Quakers in particular, 'were they numerous enough to become dangerous to the state, would
deserve the magistrate's care and watchfulness to suppress
them', largely, it seems, because of their refusal to take off
their hats. Locke even went on to suggest that if 'any
fashion of clothes distinct from that of the magistrate and
those that adhere to him should spread itself and become
the badge of a very considerable part of the people', this
might give the government reasonable cause to forbid it.

In the final version of the Essay, however, Locke deleted
these passages and substituted a markedly more permissive
one. He now rejected the idea that political security
necessitated such uniformity, lest when people form sects
they 'may occasion disorder, conspiracies and seditions,
. . . and endanger the government'. Instead he declared
that if this were so 'all discontented and active men must
be removed, and whispering must be less tolerated than
preaching, as much more likely to carry on and foment a
conspiracy'. If the formation of separate unions or corporations is not to be allowed, 'all charters of towns,
especially great ones, are presently to be taken away'; but
union in religion, he now felt sure, was no more a threat
to the government than union in the privileges of a corporation.

Locke also inserted a passage which significantly modified his earlier doctrine about indifference.

'Twill be said [he wrote] that if a toleration shall be allowed
as due to all the parts of religious worship, it will shut out the
magistrate's power from making laws about those things over
which it is acknowledged on all hands that he has a power,
viz. things indifferent, as many things made use of in religious
worship are, viz. wearing a white or a black garment, kneeling
or not kneeling, &c. To which I answer that in religious worship
nothing is indifferent, for it being the using of those habits,

gestures, &c., and no other, which I think acceptable to God in my worshipping of him, however they may be in their own nature perfectly indifferent, yet when I am worshipping my God in a way I think he has prescribed and will approve of, I cannot alter, omit or add any circumstances in that which I think the true way of worship.

Thus while Locke continued to maintain the principle that the magistrate had a right to exercise control over in-different things, in effect he excluded the whole concept of indifferency from the sphere of religion.

Though differing in form and arrangement, this essay anticipated the main arguments and conclusions of the *Epistola de Tolerantia* of 1689, and was based on the funda-mental thesis which Locke adhered to consistently all through his life. In the preface to his translation William Popple declared that 'absolute liberty, just and true liberty, equal and impartial liberty, is the thing that we stand in need of'. This, however, was going too far, for Locke never believed in 'absolute liberty'. Besides exclud-ing papists and atheists, he always gave the magistrate a right to interfere in religious matters, where peace and public order necessitated it. As he grew older, however, he undoubtedly came to lay less emphasis on the justification for interference, and more on the need for freedom of thought and worship. His biographer praises him because he 'went far beyond the most liberal of the independents' in pleading for 'the utmost freedom of opinion in religious matters . . . to all outside the limits of the national church',[1] restraining them only if their social or political views ran contrary to the true interests of the community, and also 'went far beyond the most liberal of the latitudinarian

[1] This is an exaggeration, for Locke would not have approved of the more extreme demands of some of the sectaries. He would have thought them anarchical, which indeed they were.

churchmen' in his plea for comprehension, 'so broadening the area of doctrine and so simplifying the methods of ritual appointed for the national church as to leave to most reasonable persons very little excuse indeed for refusing to belong to it'.[1]

Not everyone, however, not even the firmest believers in religious liberty and freedom of thought, would endorse the admiration implied in this account of Locke's theory. In the first place, now as much as then, there is the difficulty of accepting his notion that the essentials of religious faith could be reduced to a few broad tenets which were a kind of lowest common factor between all the Christian churches.[2] Then again, his conception of the church as a voluntary society (irrespective of any arguments which can be used in favour of the voluntary principle in the modern state) is as false historically as his theory, with which it is connected, that the origin of all societies, the state included, is in the consent of contracting individuals. His view on the nature of the church, and of the place of authority (whether clerical or secular) in religious matters, suffers too, as does his whole political and social theory, from his exaggerated belief in the capacity of the human intellect to make a rational choice in a field where historical traditions and habits, and only too often ignorant prejudices, are the dominant factors.[3]

Locke regarded himself as a churchman, but his church-

[1] Fox Bourne, op. cit., i. 167.

[2] In his *Second Vindication of the Reasonableness of Christianity* (1697) he reduced the creed to 'the believing of Jesus of Nazareth to be the Messiah', but he added that this involves 'receiving him for our Lord and King, promised and sent from God, and so lays upon all his subjects an absolute and indispensable necessity of assenting to all that they can attain of the knowledge of what he taught, and of a sincere obedience to all that he commands' (Fox Bourne, op. cit., ii. 409).

[3] Cf. A. A. Seaton, *The Theory of Toleration under the Later Stuarts*, pp. 263–8.

manship was of a very loose and unorthodox kind, in some respects exceeding even the limits of latitudinarianism; and though he never sympathized with sectarian extremism, his conception of the church, and of its relation to the state, was typical of nonconformity. Though not a separatist himself, he championed the right of separatists to form their own independent churches, and this was the root of his belief in toleration.[1] Even his intolerance of atheism was a consequence of the same belief in the right of free individuals to form voluntary societies by consent; for the atheist, in disbelieving in God, disbelieves in the author of the law of nature. Such disbelief undermines the obligation to keep promises and contracts, which is what holds society together. Atheism, therefore, is potentially anarchy.[2]

Locke's sympathy with the nonconformists, which indeed he shared with the Whig party generally, is exhibited clearly in an unpublished treatise against Edward Stillingfleet, then Dean of St. Paul's, with whom, as Bishop of Worcester, Locke was later to be engaged in a lengthy theological controversy. Lord King printed some extracts from this treatise, under the title *A Defence of Nonconformity*, explaining that Locke wrote it in answer to a sermon of Stillingfleet's against the nonconformists (1680) and to Stillingfleet's rejoinder (1683) to Presbyterian and Independent replies to his sermon.[3] This

[1] On this aspect of Locke's theory cf. F. Lezius, *Der Toleranzbegriff Lockes und Pufendorfs* (Leipzig, 1900). He points out that Pufendorf simply wanted freedom for the individual to interpret matters of faith for himself, but Locke pleaded for liberty to join in nonconformist sects.

[2] His intolerance of Roman Catholics, perhaps only to be expected of a Protestant and a Whig in seventeenth-century England, was scarcely more than the result of prejudice, but this, too, he could justify rationally, on the ground that Roman Catholics are potentially disloyal subjects of a Protestant government.

[3] Bodl. MS. Locke c. 34; Lord King, op. cit., p. 346.

explanation is not entirely correct, for Stillingfleet's rejoinder, entitled *The Unreasonableness of Separation*, was in fact published in 1681.[1] The treatise is in the Lovelace Collection, and consists of a large bundle of some 160 folio sheets. Lord King's extracts were taken from only a few sheets towards the end, and he overlooked the important fact, to which Dr. von Leyden drew attention, that while the manuscript is partly in Locke's hand, and partly in that of his amanuensis Brownover, it is mainly in the hand of James Tyrrell. It was probably written at Tyrrell's house at Oakley between 1681 and 1683.

Few modern readers would wish to read more than Lord King printed of these detailed arguments in justification of the right of dissenters from the established church to form independent churches. Their general trend is in accordance with the views that Locke had already expressed, and was to repeat in his published works. The fact that Tyrrell had the largest share in this treatise, however, is of interest, in view of their common concern about this time to reply to Filmer's *Patriarcha*. The Lovelace Collection also contains a number of letters from Tyrrell to Locke on various subjects, including the law of nature, in which they shared an interest.[2]

We thus come to the best-known of Locke's writings on toleration. The original of it he wrote in Latin, under the title *Epistola de Tolerantia*, while he was in exile in Holland, and addressed it to his Remonstrant theologian friend, Philip van Limborch. Limborch had it published, under a pseudonym, in Holland, and it was quickly translated into

[1] His original sermon against the nonconformists was published under the title, *The Mischief of Separation*. It was answered by Dr. Owen of Christ Church, Richard Baxter, and a number of others. See Fox Bourne, op. cit., i. 456.

[2] In 1692 Tyrrell published an English abridgement of Richard Cumberland's Latin work on the law of nature.

English by a Unitarian friend of Locke's, William Popple, who had it published, anonymously, under the title *A Letter Concerning Toleration*. There is no need here to summarize this famous work again, particularly as it largely reproduces, albeit in a different form, the conclusions Locke had arrived at years before, and had more than once committed to writing. Nor is it necessary to add more to what his biographers have already told us about the reception it met with, and the later *Letters* he wrote in defence of the views he had expressed.[1]

His support of toleration was not the only flank he exposed to attack from Tory and Anglican quarters, where some of his philosophical and theological opinions were branded as heretical, and it seems clear that though he was not, as he was accused of being, a Socinian, his theology was in fact what would now be called Unitarian.[2] The conclusion of this study, however, is no place to embark on a discussion of the theological controversies in which Locke was so much occupied in his later years. Historically, the battle for toleration was already almost won when the *Letter* was published, for it was impossible that the old intolerant uniformity should be maintained after the Revolution. Locke was disappointed at the time that the bill for comprehension was rejected, just as its predecessor had been at the Restoration, and the measure of indulgence actually accorded to dissenters by the so-called Toleration Act was much less complete than he would have wished. But in spite of a brief setback at the end of Anne's reign, the principle of toleration was now firmly established, and became more widely accepted as the

[1] See R. Klibansky and J. W. Gough (eds.), John Locke, *Epistola de Tolerantia, A Letter on Toleration* (Oxford, 1968), containing, besides Introduction and Notes, the Latin text with a new English translation.

[2] See H. McLachlan, *The Religious Opinions of Milton, Locke and Newton* (Manchester, 1941), pp. 69–114.

eighteenth century ran its course. To this result the reading of Locke's published work contributed its share, even though he had said nothing new. The importance of Locke's *Letter* in the history of toleration, like the importance of his *Two Treatises of Government* in the history of civil liberty, lies not in its novelty or originality, nor in any remarkable or radical liberality. His works were persuasive in their age because of their orderliness and reasonableness and philosophical temper; and these qualities they owed in no small measure to being based on lifelong convictions reinforced by years of study and reflection.

INDEX